Our Adventures in the Wild

Our Adventures in the Wild

Terry Simpson

Copyright © 2007 by Terry Simpson.

Library of Congress Control Number: 2007902853
ISBN: Hardcover   978-1-4257-5876-9
               Softcover   978-1-4257-5867-7

All rights reserved. No part of this book may be reproduced or transmitted in any form or by any means, electronic or mechanical, including photocopying, recording, or by any information storage and retrieval system, without permission in writing from the copyright owner.

This book was printed in the United States of America.

To order additional copies of this book, contact:
Xlibris Corporation
1-888-795-4274
www.Xlibris.com
Orders@Xlibris.com

38649

Contents

Acknowledgment 7
Introduction 9

Chapter 1: Bow Hunting 11
Chapter 2: Caribou 15
Chapter 3: Man's Best Friend 20
Chapter 4: Pistol Buck 23
Chapter 5: Colorado Elk 26
Chapter 6: Wyoming Elk the Hunt from Hell 30
Chapter 7: Newfoundland Moose 37
Chapter 8: Bears, Bears, Bears 43
Chapter 9: Five Ponds 47
Chapter 10: Summer of '04 51
Chapter 11: Lowes Lake 56
Chapter 12: Howland's Island 61
Chapter 13: Hudson River 64
Chapter 14: The Farm 68
Chapter 15: Canoeing 72
Chapter 16: Backpacking 79
Chapter 17: Arizona Elk 83
Chapter 18: Our Biggest Bucks 93
Chapter 19: Our Wedding 97

Acknowledgment

I would like to thank all my family and friends for making my life worth remembering and my wife, Jeni, that I love so much, who made my life worth living. I dedicate this book to you.

Introduction

The snap of a twig breaks the dead silence as dusk is taking over, and daylight is fading fast. My attention is quickly and intensely focused at three o'clock from my position. *What was that? It ain't no squirrel!* (Excuse my English.) I'm motionless, standing twelve feet up concealed in a hemlock tree and dressed in full camo. I have a definite advantage over any approaching game. The woods are dead quiet, not even a breeze moving the leaves on the trees. It's almost eerie. My heart thumps and jumps straight to my throat when motion is detected twenty-five yards away. Hardly a sound is made when it moves, so graceful, so dark—a mature whitetail moving slowly from my right to my left. A *buck,* and he's no spikehorn either. My heart is racing, and excitement is taking over. He will pass my watch at just twelve yards if I don't spook him first. He had no idea I was there when he stopped directly in front of me and looked to my twelve o'clock. Not a sound was made when I drew my compound bow and acquired my anchor point. My heart was about to explode from my chest. *Calm down, put it all together, and do it right,* I thought. The arrow sprang from its rest when my green twenty-yard pin found my point of intention just behind the shoulder. Instantly, the buck bolted when he took the hit, straight away from me and disappeared into the dark. The buck was a beautiful eight-point, two and a half years old, and one hundred seventy-two pounds.

This was just one of the many exciting moments I have experienced in the great outdoors. I have found adventure not only in hunting with a bow but with a pistol and shotgun as well as a rifle. I have explored mountains, rivers and lakes, deserts and swamps.

Who am I, you ask? I'm just a workingman like you—no rich Dad or Mom trying to give me everything I want, no company sponsor sending me on a big-game hunt for the advertising rights. No, I'm just an eight-to-five guy that enjoys the great outdoors and all that goes with it.

In the chapters to follow, you'll join me on wild-river trips. You will be there as I become engulfed with the bow and arrow, experience my first guided hunt, which was the hunt from hell. You will feel what it's like to have game so close you can almost touch them, then laugh at the light side, and enjoy the friendships I made along the way. Yes, I'm just like you.

My name is Terry Simpson. I was born in upstate New York and raised on a farm. I graduated from Belleville High School in 1965, a medic in the army reserve, and a self-employed carpenter. I have been married three times and divorced twice, but that's a whole different story. I'm currently married to the girl of my dreams, Jenny, a girl that joins me in every endeavor we chose to experience—from hunting, hiking, canoeing, and camping to traveling everywhere from Maine to Hawaii, Canada to Mexico. I have three daughters that have been tagging along and joined in all the fun. Yes, I'm just like you, so join us as we experience the adventure and enjoy the great outdoors.

Chapter 1

BOW HUNTING

It's a cold and stormy day in February. You know the song, "The weather outside is frightful, but the fire inside is delightful." Well, that's the way it is here in my cabin near the swamp, where Jenny and I live. I'm sitting at the table with a hot cup of coffee and the woodstove going with a record turnout of twenty-four deer feeding in our yard. Also, a pair of cardinals, blue jays, and chickadees at the bird feeder. This is where I relax, lean back, and remember days gone by.

Bow hunting, archery, league shooting, tournaments all over the state and Canada—how did it all begin? It was back, I mean way back, 1978 when my friend Gordy and I decided to try bow hunting because you are allowed to take buck or doe. Wow, think of that—a doe permit every year. We knew nothing about bows. We thought, *They're all the same, just buy one.* So we bought two just alike, PSE compounds and a dozen wooden arrows. It's a wonder we weren't killed, shooting wooden arrows out of a compound bow. They aren't splined to take the energy of a compound. We were lucky they didn't explode. Shortly after buying these bows, I was on a Sunday drive and located an archery shop. "Hey, stop here, yes, just what the doctor ordered." The right size bow for each individual, arrows splined for the weight you are shooting, and the right length; and what is this, sights on a bow? "Wow. You can't miss." So the archery bug bit me and bit me hard.

I began shooting a few arrows every day, my objective, to build muscle tone for shooting. It's hard to hit the target if you're shaking all over the place. I extended the quantity of arrows almost daily and with each day found a more consistent pattern. The better I got, the more excited I grew about shooting. I was restricted to just twenty-five yards at home. I lived in the village at this time and didn't figure you would shoot any farther at a deer than that anyway. I was very happy with my archery ability.

I returned to the archery shop on many occasions—you know what I mean, every chance I got, that's what I mean—to buy more toys for my newfound love. Here, I met a man that was the president of an archery club that was formed only a year ago. He invited me to shoot a round with him; maybe I'd join up. To my utter amazement, he shot at a bull's-eye the size of a quarter from just feet away to a bull's-eye the size of a softball eighty yards away. I was impressed and joined the club, known as the Dry Hill Archers. Enthusiasm struck again, I participated in their league, which shot one night a week for score. The targets were changed weekly, and there were different rounds: field round, hunter round, and the animal round. I found myself at the club at least three days a week, shooting, increasing my scores almost weekly. Three times through the course of the summer, the club had a Sunday tournament, which other clubs came to compete in. As you can gather, the archery bug not only bit me hard, it had consumed my whole body, heart, and soul.

The summer ended, and hunting season began. Hunting consumes me all fall, even more now that I hunt the early bow season. I'm always excited—you know, leave work and head for the swamp and stay in the swamp all weekend. There's no time for anything else; I've gone hunting.

With the coming of Christmas, hunting season is over; I've hung my bow on the wall and put my guns away. It's going to be a long winter before I can start shooting again. Then my life was reenergized when the club president called with news of a place to shoot indoors all winter—"Yes, I'm saved"—and about mid-January, we began indoor league, sixty arrows at twenty yards, a three hundred score possible. Again Sunday tournaments all over the state and Canada. It made the winter pass by quickly, and so the archery bug stayed with me all year long, year after year after year. My bow became part of me. I never shot less than three days a week, and sometimes I found myself shooting every day. I bought a camper trailer to travel to tournaments with. My daughter, Karen, began shooting with me; then Jenny came along, and I introduced her to the bow. If you think I had it bad before, there was no help for me now. We began traveling every weekend somewhere, shooting in whatever tournament we could find.

With archery as a big part of my family, we gave more time to the local club and really had fun setting up the local tournaments. When you traveled, you were at their mercy, so it was payback time when they traveled to your club. Animal shoots became really big, especially for the bow hunters. There were your traditional animals: deer, bear, elk, moose, fox, wolf, pig, rabbit, pheasant, squirrel, and woodchuck. And then there were the more difficult, like a butterfly, spider, or a snake wrapped around a tree. Also, a running deer, where timing was everything and the all-famous iron deer, with only the vitals cut out; a miss meant your arrow was destroyed. Terrain also came into the picture: uphill, downhill, across a gorge, a pond, or gravel pit. Look for a shot and get your arrow through a hole no bigger than a softball or by a tree covering the vital area. Remember, you must make a vital shot to get points; in some tournaments, a wound meant minus points. Also, shoot from tree stands, sometimes straight down, and this is like shooting at a quarter on edge or a deer fifty yards out. And your arrow trajectory is everything, over the limb or under it, and sometimes that sound every bow hunter hates to hear—*click, click, click.*

As the years passed, we attracted more shooters from farther away by having a two-day tournament, with awards on Saturdays and Sundays for daily top shooters and bigger awards for combined scores. The challenge cup came into play, the top three scores from your club against the top three scores of each club entered. Also, along the way, the novelty shoot helped generate more revenue for the club hosting the shoot. Through the years and all the tournaments, there are some great memories of family and friends and those really special shots you'll never forget—whether they were pure luck or some degree of skill, who knows? But you made them.

A tournament in Kingston, Canada, found us shooting at animals. This particular target was a moose at the far side of a gravel pit; the moose was a long shot, maybe fifty yards with a strong wind blowing right to left. The first two men missed him completely—as I said, a strong wind. The third man managed a gut shot. I'm last, a major downhill shot fifty yards, wind blowing. I led the animal by six feet, held my fifty-yard pin low, and let it go. The wind forced the arrow left and placed it deep in the vital area. One of the other fellows commented, "There's no stopping him today." And there wasn't.

At a two-day tournament, the last target on the course was a novelty target, a standing bear on the other side of the pond. I estimated it to be about a hundred yards away. One dollar per arrow and closest arrow to the nail in the center of the bear's chest after two days' shooting wins half the money. Jenny and I exited the course with two other shooters and were asked if we would shoot at the bear. I had three one-dollar bills in my pocket. "I'll shoot three arrows," I replied. With a spotting scope mounted on the table, they were able to inform you of the location of your arrow after your shot. There were a few onlookers to cheer or laugh whatever the case may be. My decision to shoot brought an instant response of, "I've got fifty cents that his first arrow is in the pond." "Hell, I'll bet that all three of his arrows are in the pond," came another. "Encouraging, aren't they," I replied. I estimated the distance, figured what I had to do with my pin configuration, drew, anchored, elevated my bow, held it steady, and fired. The arrow made that distinctive sound of target hit. "You're in the kill circle, six inches low and two inches to the right of the nail." I fired again, another hit. "Your left and right are perfect but still six inches low." Again I fired, and again my arrow found the inside of the kill circle. An onlooker asked, "How the hell did you do that?" I responded, "Everybody gets lucky." And after two days of shooting and over 120 arrows, Jenny won. Her arrow was closer to the nail in the bear than one-half of an inch. That's my Jenny.

When my daughter, Karen, was only fourteen years old and Stephanie was six, we went to a tournament way up in Canada. It was a very grueling course—twice around, fifty targets each round. Karen was always a stout girl so they placed her in the women's class. She objected that she was only fourteen and should be in the youth class, with no success. I told her to just shoot her best and have some fun. She did and walked away with first place and a smile I'll never forget. As for Steph, she walked all the way around that course twice and slept all the way home.

Another one of those world-class shots came at a tournament in Massena, New York. The novelty shoot was a bull's-eye target four-foot square and about two hundred yards away. Talk about total guess, I have no idea how to get that kind of elevation. All you can do is shoot a Hail Mary and hope. I paid five dollars to shoot three arrows; I figured lose three arrows but what the hell. There were fifteen men and women on the line and one pair of field glasses watching. "OK, it's clear to shoot." I placed my sixty-yard pin on the target elevated straight up, my pin hit a white spot on a cloud, and I fired. Someone just hit the bull's-eye. *The timing was about right,* I thought; so I did it again. "Blue ring," she said. It must be mine. I fired again, bottom of the target. At this tournament, I won my class, the challenge cup, and after forty-five arrows fired in the novelty shoot; the only three arrows in the target belonged to me. Must be I got lucky again.

Over the years, we continued to shoot year round to stay in shape for that all-important time of year—hunting season. The memories we have will last forever, as will our success. Karen was State Style Champion twice, and Jenny was also State Style Champion twice. As far as state competition, the best I ever did was to finish second, and the man that beat me won the nationals that year. My friends, John and Randy, and myself shot in five challenge cup tournaments in one year and won four of them. The one we lost, we lost by one point. In Niagara Falls, I won the maid of the mist tournament by one point on the last target. Our accomplishments are not only on the wall but also in our hearts and minds. We also treasure all the friends we made along the way, and it all started over hunting season.

Chapter 2

CARIBOU

My friends and I are booked to hunt caribou in early September 1988. We will hunt strictly archery on this particular hunt. The camp we are in is brand-new. This is the first season of hunting in this area. According to our outfitter, he has reserved this area for bow hunters only, and no rifles will be allowed to hunt here. We were all pleased with this ruling. It is very hard to compete with the rifle style of hunting when you are bow hunting. You may be stalking an animal with a bow, using cover and concealment and not be seen by the rifle hunter two or three hundred yards away.

We have arrived in camp by floatplane and the last group is ready to leave. They have had a good week with 100 percent success. I ask one of the fellas where is a good area to get into. He pointed to the other side of the lake. "The caribou will cross the inlet over there, with plenty of cover. You won't have any problem finding a spot where you can hear them cross the inlet." I thanked him and listened to the fella's tales about last week.

Our sprits are high; it sounds good, with their reports of all kinds of animals. With our gear stowed away in the most comfortable platform tent, we began a little scouting. I crossed the lake with one of my friends, Keith, in one of the three motorboats provided for us by the outfitter. We found many trails where caribou had left the lake and also found the inlet the previous hunters mentioned.

As we watched the most fabulous display of northern lights I have ever seen, we talked of our strategy for the coming day. Because we are allowed to take two animals of either sex, I plan to take the first animal that gives me a shot. If it's a cow, fine. At least I will have some meat for my money. I will then hunt for a bull for the remainder of the hunt.

With anticipations running high, very little sleep was gotten that first night. With the first person stirring in the early morning, we were all up. After fresh coffee and a hardy breakfast, we are ready to go.

I must add that on this hunt, we brought our own food, prepared it ourselves, and did our own dishes. We have a camp attendant; his duties are to cut the firewood and give us a hand if we need it. He told us just to wave our orange vests from the shore around the lake, and he will come to give us a hand.

Keith and I hitched a ride to the other side of the lake for our first hunt. We took up a vigil at what appeared to be an active run from the lake. Hours passed with no action in our area. Steve came to get us in the afternoon with news of the first animal on the ground. Without hesitation, we left our stands to give him a hand. We hiked to the top of a small mountain and found his game. Steve was very excited and proud of his fine bull. After taking some pictures and pats on the back, it's time to work. We skinned out the animal, quartered, and packed it down the mountain to the boat. "One down."

With Steve's animal in the meat house, we see an orange vest waving at the north end of the lake. Into a boat and north we go. It's Bill, with news of another animal down. We follow him up another mountain and dance to the story of a sixty-yard shot right on the money. A respectable bull was produced from a fantastic shot. Again, we packed the animal down to the boat to hang in the meat house. Our first day has ended with two hanging. Steve and Bill are on cloud nine, and again anticipations are running high.

Most of our evening meals were macaroni with a topping like sweet-and-sour pork or Italian sauce. Breakfast was mostly pancakes or cereal. Lunch was a pop tart or candy bar, whatever you had in your day pack when you felt the urge. One night, after an inspiring dinner of macaroni, Jim took his turn at dishes as the rest of us sat around the table with a cup of coffee, just enjoying good conversation. With the dishes done, Jim opened the front door and gave the dishwater a toss. Instantly a yell of "Hey" came from outside. Jim reached in his pocket for his glasses, put them on, and looked outside. "Keith, I'm sorry I didn't see you there." With that, Keith came through the door, shirt wet and macaroni in his hair. The tent just rolled with laughter.

Morning of Day 2

Again, everyone is up and raring to go. I decided to try over next to the inlet today. Keith opted to go in back of the camp. So I hitched a ride across the lake and headed for the inlet. I found a good spot just fifty yards from the inlet, a watch located on the east side with excellent cover and wide-open shooting for twenty-five yards. The only problem was a slight breeze hitting me in the back of the neck. The caribou might pick up my scent here, but I decided to try it anyway.

My bow for this hunt was a Pearson ZB-1, an early cam bow. Overdraw was a new feature at this time, so I was using the longest one I could put on my bow, which increased my arrow speed and flattened my trajectory. My arrows were 2013 camo XX75s armed with razorback fours. My draw weight was sixty-two pounds. and arrow speed was 229 feet per second. I could gain a little more speed with a lighter head, but, for caribou, I wanted more kinetic energy to drive the arrow through the ribs.

I hear splashing in the inlet, a white cow up on the shore and heading up the trail, which will pass directly past my watch. I'm ready, just waiting for the animal to come within range. Her forward motion was abruptly stopped, and she looked directly toward my blind. She quickly turned and headed back to the inlet. I'm sure she picked up my scent. I decided that this spot wouldn't do, so I moved across the clearing and made a blind on the other side. Now the slight breeze is in my face, and the lake is to my back. The cover here is shorter, and to remain concealed, I must shoot from my knees. Splashing in the inlet was another cow; her heading was perfect as I watched her through the cover. She approached to within twenty yards of my watch; I come to full draw. My anchor was perfect as I wait for her to step into the clearing. She entered the clearing at a moderate pace and would pass in front of me at just ten yards. My florescent pin was fixed on her front shoulder; *watch her steps, left leg out front, now.* I released the arrow, and it quickly made its mark, *thump*, as the arrow passed behind the shoulder and through both lungs. In less time than it takes to breathe, the animal disappeared in the heavy cover. "Yes! A perfect hit." I just want to jump up and yell, but my legs are killing me. Now I can get off my knees and straighten out my legs. My heart is still pounding from the adrenaline rush. *Take your time, let the arrow do its job, no need to push her into the next territory.* I picked up my day pack and began looking for my arrow. When I found it, it was covered with pink blood with tiny bubbles on the shaft, which confirmed my belief of a lung hit. Without any problem, I was able to pick up the trail and began to search. Slowly were my movements, watching the ground for evidence that she passed this way and checking in front of me to make sure I didn't spook her farther away. I followed the trail about seventy-five yards into the cover. Bingo—there she is on the ground. I dropped to one knee and grabbed my field glasses and watched for a minute; no motion, she's done. I approached slowly with another arrow loaded just in case. A slight kick with my boot, no reaction. I returned my arrow to its quiver. After taking a few pictures and completing the field dressing, I headed to the lake.

As I'm sitting on the shore, waving my vest, I notice another orange vest toward the south end. Looking with my field glasses, I saw that Keith was the other one waving. Steve grabbed a boat and came for me. We decided to check Keith out before retrieving my game. Keith had also arrowed a cow, which retreated to the lake and died about fifty yards offshore. Steve and I retrieved his game and dragged it up on the shore for him to field dress. This was Keith's first with a bow, so his excitement was at an extreme high. With pats on the back and pictures, we left him to retrieve my caribou.

On this day, Jim missed a couple and asked for some assistance to locate his problem. Of course, we help in any way we can anyone and everyone we hunt with.

The third day of our hunt would turn out to be our best day, and a day that is etched in my mind forever. I returned to the spot where I made my shot the day before. After a short lapse of time, I was hearing and seeing animals on the other side of the inlet. I decided to check it out. I had to wander upstream to a spot where I could stone jump to the other side. Sign was heavy here, heavier than where I was yesterday. I found a spot where the runs were wide and heavily traveled. Quickly throwing together a blind, I again returned to my knees. The breeze is in my face, and my bow is loaded. Soon the clicking of hooves draws my attention to several animals coming in my direction. They seem to be spooked and moving very rapidly toward me. *No bulls,* are my thoughts. I remained motionless as the animals came closer and closer, again seemingly very spooked. *Oh shit, look out!* I thought, as a cow came directly at me and passed through my blind just inches from me, and I mean inches. I could have touched her with my elbow. *I really don't think I like this spot,* I think to myself. I'll find a better place, a little less dangerous. The number of animals impressed me so I wanted to stay on the same trail. Moving in the direction the animals came from, I hiked maybe a half mile when I found a place that appeared to be a natural wall, and several trails funneled down to one opening and then fanned back out again. *Perfect spot.* I moved up a slight hill about twenty yards from the opening, planning to make a blind, when I heard the clicking of hooves and the sounds of coughing. When I located the animals, they were about fifty yards away. *Bulls.* One, two—five of them. *Quickly load your bow, cover, no time; they're headed for the opening.* Looking them over, I decided the last one was the biggest. I'm standing in the wide open, with no chance to cover my movements. In seconds, the first, second, and third animal pass through the opening. As the fourth animal enters the opening, I must draw. The fourth animal stops, and the fifth animal, the one I want, moves behind him. *Shit, no shot.* I wait motionless; the fourth animal took one step, giving me a small target behind his thigh and in front of the midsection on number 5. My pin hits the spot, and instantly the arrow is released. *Thump.* Number 4 bolts from the spot. Number 5 instantly turns to the left with two or three steps. The blood running down his side gives me a quick indication, liver. *Another shot,* is my thought. Reload, draw, anchor, spot, and shoot as the bull jumped to the left. Just nicked him. He charges through the opening and up the hill, out of sight. My heart is pounding. Don't push him, just pick up the trail and slowly stalk. Up the hill, always watching the ground in front of me. A hundred yards later, there is an animal standing in the trail sixty yards away. A big bull with his butt toward me, I'm not sure if it's the one I shot. He looks around, takes a step to the right, and bingo—blood running down his side. Draw, anchor, no shot. He moves into cover and stops, no shot. I return my arrow to its quiver and begin my approach on my hands and knees, hoping for a clear shot. As I moved to within forty yards, the big bull laid down. "You can lie right there. It's OK by me." About three minutes lapsed. To my amazement, he returned to his feet. *Shit, here we go again.* He begins to move downhill. *That's OK, you can head for the lake if you want.* And he did. Downhill we went. He traveled to within a hundred yards of the lake and went into a heap. His running was over. I approached him with caution, amazed at his mass, both body and rack. What a beast. I never dreamed I'd score on such an animal. Pictures and field dressing completed, I managed to drag the huge body the remanding hundred yards to the lake, a task that took me over an hour to complete. I put the beast in the water to keep out the blowflies. When the boat came to give me a hand, the animal was too big to fit in the boat. We had to float him across.

Back at camp, the camp attendant said he would cape him out for me, and I could have him mounted. He hangs in my living room now and will there live forever.

On this day, Jim harvested a nice animal, and Dody arrowed a monster which made Pope and Young. With an added bit of glory, Dody shoots bare bow—no sights, just instinctive.

This was truly a trip none of us will ever forget. Good times, with good friends, make great memories.

Chapter 3

MAN'S BEST FRIEND

It's been about two years since I last wrote a tale of hunting adventure. A recent chain of events has inspired me to write this article.

It was a beautiful fall day—sixty degrees, sunshine, and the opening day of deer season. A day on the calendar that most hunters spend nine months of the year looking forward to. Standing on watch with the anticipation of harvesting a fine buck, two men hear the sound of leaves rustling, twigs snapping, and deer coming. Both men raise their rifles in readiness to make their shot. Two deer appear in the open hardwoods, a doe and a single fawn. With still more noise coming, the men remain ready. Two dogs appear and seem to be on the track of the deer. Two quick shots and the dogs are dead. When asked, "Why did you shoot the dogs?" The reply was, "They were chasing deer, so I shot them. I am completely justified in my actions."

Let's talk about exactly what they did. I'm sure these dogs belonged to someone. Let's just assume they belonged to a farmer, and let's assume the same farmer owns the land on which the two men were hunting. Get my drift? This farmer is going to be real excited about letting people hunt on his land again. You wonder why there is so much posted property.

Put one more name on the antihunting list. Or the farmer could say, "Well, they shouldn't have been chasing deer, I guess. But the dogs don't belong to me; they belong to my ten-year-old son." Now what kind of an impression do you think is now imbedded in this ten-year-old's mind? "Two hunters killed my dogs. I hate them. I hate all hunters!" One more name on the antihunting list. Hell, you probably just swayed the whole family from prohunting, progun, to antigun in about three seconds. After all, where do the anti's come from, but from people directly affected by a shooting incident, whether it be a hunting incident, a shooting spree in a school yard, an armed robbery gone bad, or an assassination attempt. After all, where do you think the Brady Bill got its name? Jim Brady didn't get hurt in a car accident. Every time something like this or worse happens, we add more names to the anti list and remove them from the pro list. We have men and women in Washington fighting—yes, fighting—every day to keep our second amendment right and shit like this doesn't help.

One more scenario from that farmer: He could say, "You son of a bitch! You did what?" One week later and your dog is dead, and he never left the yard, to say nothing about chasing deer. "Vengeance is mine," sayeth the farmer.

"The dogs were chasing deer. I had every right." Maybe they were chasing deer, or is it possible that they were chasing a rabbit, and you just didn't see it? Or is it possible that a coyote was actually chasing all of them and the dogs were the hunted not the hunter? Well it is possible. The only ones who really know are the dogs, and they aren't talking. I wonder why.

"What is all the fuss about? They were just dogs." "Just dogs," you say. How many times have we heard of a dog saving a human life, tracking down a lost child, sniffing out drugs and illegal contraband, or a police dog sacrificing his life to save his partner? Just a dog. He's been known as man's best friend for as long as I can remember.

A man told me, with tears in his eyes, of the last time he and his dog went hunting. They hunted for birds on a fall day just one year ago. His dog, a springier spaniel, had his nose to the ground, looking for birds. Never far, not more than thirty yards at any time, any farther would be too long a shot. Then a shot rang out and his dog yipped. He called his name and ran to the dog's side just in time to hear him take his last breath. He was dead, shot just thirty yards from his owner. A man came over and admitted he shot him because a week ago, he saw a dog chasing deer. Then today he saw this dog, so he shot him with not a deer in sight. The real tragedy here was that the dog was this man's family. A single man, living alone with his dog. This man spent more time with his dog than most men spend with their children. You never saw one without the other. Just a dog. No man has the right to shoot a dog, even if he is chasing deer! Who appointed you judge, jury, and executioner? The chances of a dog catching a deer during hunting season, in the peak of its physical condition, are slim and none. The real truth might be that he hadn't seen anything all day and had to kill something, and the dog showed up. Wrong place, wrong day.

Let's, for conversation's sake, say that our original two dogs had finished rounding up the farmer's cows and decided to do a little sport hunting and chase a deer or two. They're having a good time, on a good hunt, then all of a sudden, along come these two animal rights activists and ruin their hunt. And according to the animal rights activists, they were justified. Now turn things around, take the two activists and make them the hunters on a three-thousand-dollar western hunt, having a good time chasing a mule deer or an elk or two, when along come the animal rights activists and chase away all the animals and ruin their hunt. The hunters are pissed right off and just want to hurt someone. Get my drift? It all depends on what foot the shoe is on.

Take this scenario for debate. You're driving by a 7-11 store when a small-built man in a ski mask comes running out and down the street. You're sure he just robbed the store. As sure as you were about the dogs chasing deer. You make a quick decision and swerve your car and hit the small-built man and disable his getaway. You're a hero, justified in your actions because he just robbed the store. When in fact it was a kid late getting home and because he had a cold, his mother made him wear a ski mask. And it's still possible the dogs were chasing a rabbit!

We have a very rare right to keep and bear arms, a right most countries don't have. It's our duty as gun owners to protect this right by respecting the rights of others, the right to own property without the threat of losing that property to someone who felt justified in their actions. Only a police officer or conservation officer has the right to shoot a dog, who has been witnessed chasing deer. Let's leave the police work to the policemen.

One final note, after reading this article, what would the hunter say? Probably, "I'd do it again tomorrow!" And what would the farmer say?

Chapter 4

PISTOL BUCK

With the days getting shorter, and the mornings cool, I received my party's permit application in the mail. Which is a real good sign that hunting season is just around the corner. This season will be a little different. One of my hunting friends, Steve has been transferred from New York to Ohio, a distance you just don't drive on the spur of the moment. As was the case one cold morning in November a couple of years back.

Steve called and wanted to get together for an afternoon hunt. I responded with, "Sure, come on down." I live near a swamp that's two miles wide and four miles long and have hunted there since I was sixteen years old. It's a fabulous place, very tough to hunt. Not like hunting hedgerows or open fields. Here, the cover is thick, and most of your shots are close; that's another reason I hunt mostly with a bow or pistol. I have many stands in different areas of the swamp—some ridges, some bogs, or just places I know deer travel. Steve was bringing a rifle down today so I decided to put him in a hardwood stand near a hemlock ridge. Here he will be able to see a hundred yards without much trouble. I will carry my pistol and still hunt the ridge and possibly move the deer past his stand.

Upon Steve's arrival, we drank a cup of coffee and I told him of my plan for the afternoon. He agreed, though it sounded good. As I mentioned before, it is cold today so Steve has on his heavy orange coveralls so he can sit the stand. My clothing is jeans, a shirt, and an orange vest. I expect to be walking. All of this would change.

I drove us to my property in the swamp, loaded our guns, and walked to the stand we had discussed. The stand was up about twenty feet in the limbs of a white ash tree. Steve made two attempts to get into the stand without success. He returned to the ground and said it was too high, and he just wasn't comfortable; was there another alternative? My response was, "Sure,

I'll go up the tree and you walk it off." He agreed, so I told him where to go to begin his stalk and what the compass reading would be. "If you still hunt this ridge right it will take you all afternoon before you get back to here." With that, Steve left, and I climbed the tree and began my watch.

I carry an Interams .44 Magnum with a 7.5-inch barrel and a 4-power Leupold scope under my arm; here the scope stays dry and clear. I also carry a small pair of field glasses in my vest pocket, which I use to be sure of my target before I draw my gun. About three hours has passed with only about thirty minutes of daylight left, and I'm cold. I'm wondering where Steve could be. He should be coming into view soon. Just then, I spotted movement just out of the hemlocks. Without hesitation, I glassed the area and picked up a doe. Watching her with the naked eye, I thought, *I spotted bone*, so I checked her again with the glasses. *Nope, just a doe.* I continued scanning the area for more action. Did I say I was cold? I mean, I'm freezing my butt off. I didn't see any other movements except the doe, and again I thought I saw bone. So I checked her one more time, and I'll be—there's a buck on the other side of her. I continued watching the two of them move from my left to my right about a hundred yards away. Steve appears on the edge of the hemlocks with no hat on and his coveralls wide open. He's cooking, and I'm freezing. The sweat is rolling off him, and I'm shaking like a leaf. I'm so cold. Steve looked my way, and I gave him a signal to go around, and he disappeared back into the hemlocks. I placed my glasses in my pocket and drew my pistol and began watching the pair through the scope of the pistol. The two remained quite still with no real opportunity to make a shot. The doe begins to move, leaving the buck, and walks in my direction. She passes my tree at about twenty yards. I'm sure the buck will follow. *No such luck.* The buck approached to about eighty yards and did an about-face. "Shit, it's now or never; he's going to spook." My thumb reaches for the hammer, three quick clicks, and realign the scope; he's looking straight away, break his back. It's my only shot. With the adrenaline pumping, the shivering has stopped. With no bench rest, I must make my shot completely off-hand. I placed the crosshairs on his back just behind the shoulders; and without another thought, my gun roared, and the buck went down. With daylight fading fast, I called to Steve to locate my game while I remained in the stand. Everything seems to change when you hit the ground; you're not so sure of the location anymore. Steve appeared and I directed him to my buck. He was truly amazed when he located him. I asked him, "How far was that shot?" "A good eighty yards," he responded. I climbed down from my stand and made my way to Steve, and I want to tell you that I'm cold. I'm so cold I'm shaking. I can't even hold the knife. So Steve did the honors while I warmed up. After all, he wasn't cold at all.

"That was one hell of a shot you made on him." "Well, everybody gets lucky once in a while," I responded.

The buck was a small eight point, and his rack has its place on my wall to help me remember the good times. I later paced off the distance, to discover it was seventy-two yards, which only shows that practice can make the difference. We made our drag to the truck after the daylight had left the swamp and marked the end of another great day with a great friend.

Chapter 5

COLORADO ELK

It's 1:00 AM, and Jenny and I are on an Amtrak passenger train headed for Glenwood Springs, Colorado. As the train rolls over the tracks, memories of our last trip to Colorado are eminently clear.

It was a vacation of vacations, three trips rolled into one. We left home on a road trip that would take us on a northern route through Canada from the Thousand Islands to Soute St. Marie, across part of the Badlands, where Theodore Roosevelt hunted buffalo. Here now lies the Theodore Roosevelt National Park and Teddy's cabin. Teddy Roosevelt was a man of vision. He could see that in time there would be no more wilderness areas and initiated our national park system to preserve such beauty for generations to come.

Our route then took us over the Beartooth Highway, switchback after switchback, winding up the mountain and past an array of colors from water, rocks, and trees. A fabulous ride that words cannot capture. At the top of the mountain was a sign pointing to the Beartooth, a tooth-shaped rock on the other side of the valley. As we are glassing the area, my thoughts are of early travelers and their covered wagons. How did they ever traverse these mountains?

The road led us through Cook City, a town whose clock of time stopped a hundred years ago. From there on into Yellowstone National Park, Jenny and I were here just three short days, hardly enough time to cram such natural beauty into. Breathtaking was the Grand Canyon of Yellowstone, with its upper and lower falls. I've never seen so many colors as those that surrounded the geyser trail around Old Faithful, and the engineering alone of the Old Faithful Inn was amazing. We filmed herds of bison and elk; captured shots of mountain goat, coyote, and deer; and laughed as we watched chipmunks and crows steal a bite of food around the tables at a concession stand. In my opinion, Yellowstone is a must-see for everyone. It's not just for the hiker, hunter, camper, and fisherman. It's beauty beyond words, I wish everyone could behold.

We traveled on into the Grand Teton with weather at its worst, with rain and snow. We were unable to enjoy the area as we did Yellowstone. Next through Jackson Hole and on to Colorado.

We plan a short stay at Keith and Jaime's ranch near Dotzero. Imagine a three-and-a-half-mile driveway over a mountain to a ranch house in a small valley on the other side. The ranch backs up to BLM land (Bureau of Land Management) with plenty of land available to hunt and explore. Short walks and fence-line work on the ranch have capture sightings of deer, elk, bear, and mountain lion for Keith and Jaime.

Jenny will leave me now for her trip to Florida through Branson, Missouri, with her mother, while Keith and I will pick up our bows and gear to team up with Steve and Jim for a week of elk hunting. That leaves Jaime; well, someone has to work and feed the dog.

Keith and I head for Oak Creek and the Flat Tops. We meet our guide at a trailhead where we pack the horses for a short trail ride up the mountain to camp. There were wall tents, two for hunters with sheepherder's stoves for heat and cots to sleep on. There was one guide tent, a cook tent, and—you won't believe this—a shower tent. Heaven, pure heaven.

On this hunt for elk, we were going to try a new strategy for elk we had never tried before, stand hunting. The stands are already up with trail markers to lead the way. My stand, called the cave stand, perched me in an evergreen on a small valley with a run to the east and two to the north. Steve was on top of a ridge with good sign passing his stand, Jim on a side hill overlooking a major runway, and Keith at the bottom, where it all comes together. After three days of stand hunting and little action, a couple of cows and some mule deer, we decided it's time to go after them. We armed ourselves with bugles, cow calls, and field glasses and headed for Bear Gulch, a distance referred to as quite a hike. So fix your day pack; we're leaving early.

Breakfast is over, and, still very dark, our guide points the way and tells us what to look for. He said the elk are probably in the dark timber. You can't drive them out so find a spot and wait. The trail there was demanding, especially for men from the east. Once at the Gulch, Steve and Jim went one way, and Keith and I went another. We hunted the day in the dark timber, moving elk but never able to get a shot. It was exciting to hear them but disturbing to be so close and yet so far away. On this particular day, I was wearing an odometer, and, at the end of the day when I took my boots off, I had walked more than nine miles, and none of it was on the level.

At dinner, the next day's plans were laid, and Steve and Jim opted to hit the stands again while Keith and I would stuff our packs for another day in Bear Gulch.

I began bugling just after daybreak with a good response across the valley. Glassing the other side, we caught sightings of several elk in the oak brush, feeding on acorns. We watched the elk leave the dark timber and travel through the aspen and into the oaks.

"Wow, did you see that? Holy shit, he's a monster! Just look at the rack on him!" Our excitement soars as we plan our strategy, hike around the valley, and get the wind in our face. I will sneak into the aspen, and Keith will still hunt the oak brush and possibly get a shot. If not, then hopefully they will pass through the aspens close to me as they head back into the dark timber. We made the ridge, painted our faces and hands with camo paint, and split up. I passed two nice runs and came to a ridge, with a hot run running along the ridge and one on the other side. I took up residence under an evergreen and made ready. Noise at my back. I turned forty-five degrees and picked up a calf. As I watched it for a while, it slowly moved off into the dark timber. Limbs are cracking in the dark timber just thirty yards away, but I can't see anything. "Come out of there, show yourself." Time passes as I listen and watch, waiting for something I can lay my eyeball on. My heart rate jumps when a whistle comes from my right. "Oh no, it's Keith." The elk are on my left as Keith slowly and cautiously comes into view, whistles again, and with that comes the crash of timber and the thunder of hooves. The expression on Keith's face was truly one of "I'm sorry." Oh well, if it were easy, where would the challenge be?

We decide to leave the area and not give chase. They will be back tomorrow if we don't drive them out of the state today, and we'll bring Steve and Jim with us. I already had spots picked out in my mind for everyone to cover all the aspens, where the elk passed through. Keith and I left the area as quietly as we could and went back to camp. Excited about tomorrow, we talked over dinner of our plans. Steve and Jim agreed it sounded good and would surely join us.

The morning came, bringing great weather with it. We made the hike, and I quickly put Jim between the first two runs going down into the valley. Steve took up vigil—where the calf went into the dark timber, myself under the evergreen as I was yesterday, and Keith over the ridge on the next run.

It wasn't long before things started to happen. Jim had two cows pass by him, both within range, but he wanted a bull. Keith heard a snap, looked over his shoulder at a nice bull, made his swing, and drew all in the same motion. The elk stopped, and when Keith's pin hit the shoulder, the arrow was released. In his words, "The arrow was headed straight for its mark. He was mine, meat on the table," until *click*—as most bow hunters experience—that one branch, the one twig between you and immortality. Your heart stops, your mind goes blank as your game disappears, and all you can say is, "Shit."

Soon it's my turn, and the noises begin to my left again in the dark timber—limbs cracking, hooves hitting the earth, and then this ear-piercing bugle just inside the dark timber. The hair stands up on my neck, my heart is pounding, and I begin to shake. I'm shaking so bad I'm afraid my arrow will fall off its rest. This has never happened before. I'm not sure I have the strength to draw my bow. "Where is he?" He bugles again. "He's right there." "Where? I can't see him." He bugles again and again. Now he's moving toward Steve and still bugling. Not knowing what to do, I remained at my post. Steve, about a hundred yards to my rear, catches his rack over the brush; and in his words he said, "He is huge." As the elk lifted his head to bugle again, Steve moved to try for a shot, the elk spotted him and turned to retreat. Steve caught a motion to his left. Another bull. Steve turned, drew, and released his traditional bow and arrow in less time than it takes to blink. His arrow went deep into the elk's chest, just behind the shoulder, and disappeared into the dark timber. The huge bull retraced his steps back by me and was gone.

With time to think, I should have known the bull might detect Steve and return where it was safe. I should have left my post and moved into the dark timber, anticipating what actually happened. The action was so intense for the whole two minutes that I couldn't think. I couldn't even move. Steve waited awhile, gathered his thoughts and then came for me. In a loud whisper, I said, "Did you hear him?" Steve nodded his head yes. "Did you see him?" Again, yes. "Did you get a shot?" Again, yes. "Did you hit him?" With his eyebrows lifted high, he nodded his head—yes, yes, yes! "All right, let's go!" As I came from my post, Steve told me of the chain of events. We quietly entered the dark timber in the same place the elk did. I quickly picked up the trail. Steve found his arrow; the blood had rings of air bubbles on the shaft, a great sign. We trailed him for about a hundred yards and then were unable to determine his direction of travel. Steve opted to go for help at camp to aid in tracking. I left the area and waited for his return. With Keith, Jim, myself, and the guide, we again returned to track. Keith found more sign beyond our last spot. With a heading again, I quickly picked up the trail that led to Steve's game, a fine four by three taken with traditional equipment, a real trophy. Steve is on cloud nine, as he should be. With pictures taken, the work begins, and the animal is quartered and packed back to camp—where it's time to celebrate, laugh, and tell the story of another great trip.

Although the content of this story is true,
some of the names have been changed to protect the author.

Chapter 6

WYOMING ELK THE HUNT FROM HELL

It was Sunday morning, around 11:00, and my tent was down, sleeping bag rolled up and all my hunting gear packed away. The last horse to be packed was in camp. As one of the guides began tying the gear on, the horse backed into a set of elk antlers nailed on a tree. All hell broke loose. Hooves went into the air as the horse squealed in pain. Men began jumping out of the way, as the horse bucked and tossed gear in every direction. Mud chunks went by me like missiles. The rail fence rattled, and other trees shook from the abuse dished out by the packhorse. Colorado, one of the guides, finally got the horse's attention and calmed her down. I looked at Jen after this fracas and said, "Can anything else happen?" I mean, it had been one thing right after another.

It was maybe midsummer 1989 when Dody, Bill, and I wanted to book our elk hunt with, we'll say, the outfitter from Wyoming. We had studied many, many brochures, narrowed it down to about six guides, and talked with them and their references before we decided this was who we would use for our first archery elk hunt. We were a party of five men and one woman, all very accomplished archers in hunting and tournament archery.

In December 1989, all of us applied for our 1990-nonresident hunting license. The draw was March of the next year, and all of us were drawn. On September 19, 1990, we left our little town of Adams, New York, for the two-thousand-mile drive to Sheridan, Wyoming. The drive was completely uneventful, with two trucks and five drivers, and we hit our destination right on schedule, 7:00 PM, Friday. Our motel rooms were awaiting us. Larry came in that evening by plane because he only had one week's vacation and couldn't drive out and back with us. We were to meet the guide Saturday morning at breakfast, and according to our brochure, we were to be ready to head up the mountain at 2:00 PM.

We met the outfitter as planned and had breakfast. I mentioned that we would be ready to go up the mountain at 2:00 PM like the brochure had said. He commented that he didn't know anything about that. He didn't want to take us up the mountain then because we would get there after dark, so he would take us up Sunday morning instead. This being the case, we had all day to kill. We took a ride around the countryside and saw literally thousands of antelope, quite a few mule deer, and some nice scenery. We also went to a museum of the Battle of the Little Big Horn, and did some shopping in the local sporting-good stores.

Sunday morning arrived, and we were all set to leave. The trucks were loaded, and we were checked out of the motel. As the morning dragged on and no one showed up to get us, we drove over to the guide's house. His wife was there, but he wasn't, and she said we could wait for him if we wanted. As the afternoon was a very long and drawn-out situation, we began to get very uneasy. It was late in the day when the guide's wife came back, and I asked about the whereabouts of the guide. "He should have been here a long time ago," she said. She offered to take us to the base of the mountain. My comment was, "That would be great." After leaving town and headed for the mountains, I had Jen's blazer flat-out and just kept her in sight, traveling better than eighty miles per hour at times.

Driving on those back roads was quite a ride, but I managed to keep her in sight all the way.

When we arrived at the base of the mountain or trailhead, if you wish, there were a couple of trucks there. These belonged to the hunters that were there last week, and they were not down yet. It wasn't long, though, before some horses were coming down the mountain and a horse trailer was coming up the road. We assisted the fellows in unloading their gear and talked about their hunt and the elk they saw. They didn't use a guide but just used the camp and horses and hunted on their own. They seemed like real nice guys but were unsuccessful in their hunt.

The horse trailer was now empty of horses, packs, and saddles. As we assisted the guides in saddling horses, it was brought to my attention by Jeni that we were two horses short. The guide couldn't figure how he did that, but, nonetheless, two people had to walk up; and while you were walking, you might as well drag a packhorse with each of you. I decided I would walk, and one of the guides was going to bring the other horse and come with me. When we were finally ready to go, with everything loaded, it was dark. So instead of leaving at 2:00 Saturday and getting to the top at dark, we didn't even start until after dark Sunday.

I'm really not sure just how far it was, but it was somewhere in the neighborhood of four miles. The guide thought it would only be a Sunday stroll. This was going up, and I mean up in the dark in a totally strange country with absolutely no idea what it was like three feet to the right, if you get my gist.

We managed to get to camp just about midnight, put our gear in the tents, and went to bed with the attitude that we finally got here. At least tomorrow we could hunt.

The next morning, it was daylight when I woke up. No one else was moving very fast. The cook hadn't arrived yet, and we were short one guide. We were supposed to have one guide for every two hunters, so one of the guides cooked us breakfast and gave us sandwich material for us to make our lunch. With this out of the way, we got ready to go out for our first morning hunt.

Because we were one guide short, we went three on one the first day. Jeff, Jeni, and I went with guide number 2, or we'll call him Buck. Bill, Dody, and Larry went with Colorado. We went just outside camp about two hundred yards and broke out of the lodge pole pines. Buck said, "Just work your way down off this mountain toward that knob and just beyond the valley there is a spring. I'll meet you there for lunch and check for sign down through there." We said we would spread out and meet him there. Buck then left Jeff, Jeni, and me. "This isn't the way I thought it would be," I said. "Nor us, either," replied Jeff and Jeni. "We'll see you at noon." As I slowly moved over the terrain, trying to digest everything I saw, I ran into Jeff. He mentioned he just saw Buck a short while ago, and he mentioned that the way back to camp was between those two rocks. *I'll remember that*, was my thought, and we parted again. Well, the morning passed, and it was close to noon as I thought I must find the spring, but I couldn't see the knob off the valley anymore because I was in the valley.

Walking up the valley, I found a little stream, so I followed it upstream to the spring, and there I found Jeff and Jeni. We had our lunch and discussed our hunt so far. Jeni mentioned she almost got knocked off her horse by a tree limb that she never saw because of the darkness the night before. Jeff said Buck told him that he arrived here from Pennsylvania yesterday. I said, "That's a day after we did, and he's supposed to know where the elk are." Before we finished lunch, Buck showed up and asked us what we had seen. None of us had seen any really good sign; so in the afternoon, we would move across this entire ridge with one at the top, one in the middle, and one at the bottom.

We would come to an escar and follow it to the bottom. He would meet us there. "Okay, but how long will it take?" was my remark. "It will take you all afternoon to get there." I took the top, Jeff took the middle, and Jen took the bottom.

As I walked across this ridge, I found what I called great sign—big rubs on trees, the ground all torn up, and droppings everywhere. My thought was, *Wow, look at this area. Okay, what do I do with it? This really isn't what I expected.* As the afternoon wore on, I finally found the escar. I followed it to the bottom and found Buck waiting there. I asked if he had seen Jeff or Jen, but his answer was "No, not yet." Jeni and I have a certain whistle we use when hunting, and that was passed on to the others early on. My feet were killing me when I got to Buck from walking on that hillside, so I removed my boots for a while when I heard Jen whistle. It was very faint, and it was beyond the spot we were supposed to meet, so Buck went to find her. She had gone beyond the escar and was headed back when she knew she had gone too far. Buck got her attention, and she wondered over where I was, but no Jeff yet.

As it started to get dark, I built a signal fire, hoping to get Jeff's attention wherever he was, but still no Jeff. With darkness rapidly approaching, Buck said, "Stay here and keep the fire going. I'll go back to camp, and if Jeff is there, I'll get a couple of horses and come back for you. If he isn't, I'll get more fellows and horses and come back to look for him. It won't be more than three hours." Jeni and I gathered more firewood and kept whistling as the night quickly set in, and the wind began to blow. As Jen and I sat by the fire, I mentioned I saw an elk carcass, not far away and bears, had been feeding on it, which made me uncomfortable. The wind blew so hard that we were unable to have a fire big enough to keep warm because I was afraid of setting the whole hillside on fire.

After four hours went by, I said he was not coming back, so we should try to get out of this wind. But when I stood up, I almost fell down because the hillside was so steep. We couldn't go anywhere because of the steepness, so I gave Jen my extra clothes that I had in my day pack, and I put on my Gor-Tex. I put Jeni tight to the rocks around the fire, then I wrapped myself around Jen to break the wind, and about every half hour or so, we put another stick on the fire; and that's the way we spent the night on the side of the mountain, the last week of September with no food, tent, or sleeping bag.

By morning, the wind had subsided, and we had a better fire to warm up with. When Buck returned, he brought good news that Jeff had made it back to camp the day before. He also brought along Larry and something for us to eat. By the time we finished breakfast, the outfitter, along with guide number 3—we'll call him Bull—and a fellow who was in camp just to take pictures, rode in on horseback. Jen's knee was bothering her from the previous day, so she decided to go back to camp. I was here to hunt, so I continued on with Larry and Buck.

The plan for this day was for me to go up the south face on the next mountain with Larry up the east face and Buck up the north face and meet on the second rock at the top at noon. Again, this was not the way I thought it should be done, but not everyone understand my work either.

Through the course of the morning, I again found what I thought to be fresh sign and again. "What do I do with it?" I tried doing a little cow calling, but unsure of my technique, I was sure my efforts were in vain. As noon approached, I found my way to the first big rock, then on up to the second. There I sat and had lunch and waited for the others, and that was where I was sitting when the sun went down on day 2 of my elk hunt.

As you can imagine, about this time, I'm not a very happy camper or hunter for that matter. I really don't know where camp is, but by the time I stop walking, I'm going to be one whole hell of a lot closer than I am right now. I had no intention of spending another night on the side of this mountain with no food, tent, sleeping bag, or company this time; so back down the mountain I went after leaving a note on the rock in case they ever did show up. I went back to where I spent the night before, and then I headed up the valley toward the spring where we had had lunch the day before. As I moved through the valley, I saw the two rocks Jeff had pointed out the day before and knew I was on the right track. I had been moving at a very rapid pace for about two hours now, and my light was fast leaving me, and the grade was getting steeper. I kept going up and up; and then, as I moved into the tree line, my light was gone. I was sure camp was somewhere in this stand of pine; then, I heard a familiar whistle. I returned the call, and it came again, but I was so tired; rather than whistle, my comment was, "Where the hell are ya?" Jeni says, "Oh no, not another good day." Nope, so just take me to camp.

Back at camp, I put my gear in my tent and washed my hands and face when Larry and Buck showed up, surprised to see me. "How long have you been here?" "I just got here. Where were you?" I asked. Buck and Larry were on the second big rock from the top, and I was on the second big rock from the bottom. My error I guess but, nevertheless, another wasted day. Talking with the other fellows around the camp fire, Bill, Dody, and Larry walked about eighteen miles the first day right out in the middle of a prairie, and Colorado started bugling. Bill was not impressed by this move at all. Dody was the only one who would hunt with Colorado after that. Colorado also came from Texas a week before our hunt. He too was well schooled on where the elk were.

Jen expressed to me that she wanted to hunt with Bull on Wednesday. He was pointing out different sign to her on their way back to camp that morning. I talked to Bull and found out he was a contractor until he broke his back. Now all he can do is walk and ride a horse and spends a lot of time here in the mountains. *My kinda guy*, I thought. So when Bull asked me if I wanted to go with him and Jeni on Wednesday, I said yes.

I was the first to arise Wednesday around 4:00 AM, washed up, changed camo, had a quick cup of coffee, and a bite too eat. When we got to where Bull wanted to start hunting, he put Jeni on the left of him and me about a hundred yards to her right. He was between and in back of us. With a signal system, we knew when to move, when to stop, and when to stay put; and he did the calling. Moving up a valley, his calls were answered.

The valley was narrow and tight, and the answer was on top. We moved to the rim, and it was bare rock for about fifty yards. We had no cover where we were, so we decided to move into the tree line. When we got inside the tree line, no one saw anything. I told Jen to get behind a blowdown to the right, and I would move to the left, and Bull would remain here. Before Jeni got behind the blowdown, I saw an elk right in front of me, about fifty yards away, looking right at me. I turned my head to Jeni. "Pisst, pisst." No response from her, and he's still looking at me. "Pisst, pisst," Jeni looks my way. I look at the elk. Jeni knows what I want and also finds the elk. I looked at her twice more, and it doesn't appear she is doing anything. Thinking someone has to do something, I decided to take one step to my left behind a tree. Bad move. The elk tipped his head back to turn around. His horns went all the way past his rump. Bull began cow calling to turn him back to us but to no avail. There were several elk with him, and they all moved on ahead of us. We spread out and slowly moved and called in their direction but were unable to make contact with them again that day. Jeni said she was ready to draw when the elk turned to move out. I didn't see that anything was happening and thought somebody better do something but, as I said, bad move.

Jeni and I were both real pleased with Bull's way of hunting and his ability to put us into elk the first time out. On Thursday, there was no sign of elk for us, but Larry had a shot and would go after him Friday morning.

Bull, Jeni, and I left camp early Friday, again hunting in our same manner, and again Bull's calls were answered directly in front of me. Bull continued to call, and the elk also continued to answer. The answer starting to move to my right and come closer, and as Bull continued to call, my heart began to pump as the adrenalin was on the move. I caught sight of a cow elk about two o'clock from my position. There was a small ridge directly to my right. I just knew the elk would appear on that knob. I turned my body on my knees and held by bow ready to draw and waited. All at once, I hear voices, voices coming down the trail. All movement seems to stop, and I hear nothing. Then the thunder of disappearing elk filled the air. *Shit*, were my thoughts as I could hear men on horses going down the trail to get to the area where Larry took his shot the night before. Oh well, just one more event in this unforgettable hunt. Again, we pursued with no luck. Larry's luck was about the same. All they found was one drop of blood, no elk. On this day, Jen fell and hurt her knee again. She was only seven weeks from her knee operation, so she was a little tender at times.

Saturday was the last day to hunt. Jen was still sore, so Bull and I went alone but were dry. Bill and Jeff decided not to hunt with any guide after Monday. Bill had blisters on his feet after his eighteen miles, and Jeff couldn't find us Monday afternoon, so he did what I did on Tuesday and tried to find camp. I was glad he did.

During the period of time from when we booked our hunt and the time we went, the man we had booked with developed heart problems and told me he wouldn't be there. He said this other man would take care of us, a man I was led to believe had been with him for years. But the truth was, the business was sold; and in my opinion, the new fellow just didn't have it all together yet—from not enough horses, to not enough food, to leaving me on the mountain, to tracking up the whole mountainside, and scaring away the elk. Other than that, it was a hunt of a lifetime, and one I'll never forget.

Chapter 7

NEWFOUNDLAND MOOSE

It's the fifteenth of September; the weather is shit, wind is blowing hard with rain turning to snow. It's cold. Tony and I have covered miles and miles since dawn when we spotted a nice bull from a spot they call the phone booth. Since then, it's been move through the black spruce and yellow bogs, trying for position. It's now one hour before dark, we're 450 yards from him, wind at our backs, and the bull is behind a tree deep inside the tree line looking our way. We agreed it's impossible to get any closer before he's gone. With my day pack on a rock, I have a good bench rest. With the tree directly in front of the bull, my only shot is to ricochet off the rock to his left. In a whisper, Tony said, "You better shoot. Their horns fall off tomorrow." And my 06 roared. If you don't believe that, then I guess I'll have to tell you the truth.

It's been thirty-five years since my good friend Ned and I graduated high school. Ned chose a career in teaching, and I in carpenter work. His career took him away from home, and we lost touch over the years. Now he has retired and purchased a nonworking farm back home. We have again become close friends and enjoy spending time together. Our wives enjoy each other as well. On one occasion, Ned implied that his life's dream was to go on a moose hunt in Newfoundland and asked me if I had any interest in going. I'm sure you know what my response was, and the research began.

First, Ned started checking the Internet, getting the names of outfitters that claim a quality hunt with comfortable accommodations and a high-success rate. I made several phone calls to references and compared the reports I had made. We made our decision to book with an outfitter called Viking Trails, who claimed 100 percent success with good accommodations, showers, flush toilet, a kitchen with a cook to prepare all our meals, and a one-on-one guide service.

It was totally impossible to go in 02, so we sent our deposit for an early-September 03 hunt with Viking Trails.

What happened after that you are not going to believe. It seemed like Wyoming all over again. It began after the United States invaded Iraq to drive out Saddam Hussein and his government. Our Canadian neighbors figured we were in the wrong. Ned e-mailed Viking Trails to see if we would still be welcome come fall. To his surprise, his e-mail was returned, no such address found. "Oh, shit!" Right. He then checked the Web page for the outfitter and acquired a new phone number. This number connected us to Leonard, the owner of Portland Creek. After talking with him, our minds rested a little easier. He explained that he had purchased Viking Trail property and would honor our reservations in September even though he had not received our deposit yet. We were, to say the least, a little nervous. We had sent our deposit and also booked our flights, which were nonrefundable. Then came mad cow when the United States closed its borders to any meat coming from Canada. Ned called our senator, our congressman, and the USDA (United States Department of Agriculture), and no one had any definite answers. All they would say was, "There is no date set to lift the ban so call closer to your hunt." Again, we called Leonard for information on our options. I asked if he could store our meat for us until the ban was lifted. He explained he didn't have the facilities for that. "Well, how about we reschedule for next year?" Again, he explained that if the Americans don't come, it will ruin me, and there won't be a next year.

Three weeks before our hunt, the moose ban was lifted, and our hunt was on again. We made a few purchases just for the hunt and took our guns to the gunsmith. Ned needed a new scope for his, and I haven't had mine out of the cabinet for at least ten years. All of my hunting has been with the bow or pistol, and everyone I talked to said your shot will be 250-plus yards. So the bow was pretty much out of the question. When we got our guns back, the gunsmith had even sighted them in for 200 yards with 180 gr. partition bullets. Ned checked his, and I also checked mine, right on at two hundred yards. The only thing left was to pack and head for Ottawa Airport. We didn't have any trouble with our weapons at the border; just show them your paperwork and hand them your money, and you're on your way. Again, no problem at the airport, locked gun case and ammo separately packed in our luggage.

On Wednesday, before we flew, we talked to Leonard one last time and told him we would arrive in Deer Lake at 4:30 Saturday and assumed we were all set. So you can imagine our surprise when no one met us at the airport. "Oh darn it," replied Ned. "I'll call." He got a response of shock when he told Leonard we were at the airport, so he sent us a cab who took us for a two-hour ride to a motel, where we spent the night. And again, we were concerned that we had made another Wyoming mistake.

Sunday morning, it all turned around when Shelly came with our hunting licenses. She was really nice and gave us our paperwork and assured us we would be in camp by the afternoon. This was the best news we have heard in nine months. Leonard himself picked us up, gear and all, and took us to our plane.

We left the lake and flew over the Newfoundland landscape at about 2,500 feet, and I want to tell you I loved it! This is a land ripped by the glaciers—now covered with black spruce, yellow bogs with small lakes, and rolling hills. The moose were introduced here in early 1900s or late 1800s with a population now of 112,000 animals. Woodland caribou also roam this land with numbers of about 80,000 animals. Of course, there is also the black bear roaming around.

George, our pilot, landed on Graydon Lake. Ned and I were met at the dock by Gerald, Mick, and Tony. The plane was quickly unloaded and sent back. We watched as he took off, circled, and flew out of sight. We are finally here; three years in the planning and obstacle after obstacle, all the hurdles have been cleared. We can now relax and enjoy our long-awaited moose hunt. Camp is only about seventy yards up the boardwalk. There, we were greeted by the cook, Mona, a lady who created miracles in her kitchen—all the way from pancakes to cheesecakes and everything in between. The rest of the afternoon was spent on top of the hill at the lookout called the phone booth, glassing the yellow bogs, looking for animals. "Got one, got two," spoke Mick, "a cow and calf in the yellow bog, east of the lake, off the point." The conversation at the booth was encouraging; all about the animals they have seen since they opened the camp. Ned and I are the first hunters this season, so our chances are good. I'm sure they can get us a shot; it will be up to us whether we take it or pass.

As the sun slowly closed the day, we wandered down the hill back to camp, where Mona fixed a cold plate for supper and talked of past hunts over a game of cribbage. Oh, the camp life, in my mind, there's nothing better. Laughter filled the room, and anticipations were on the rise. "Man, oh man, it's great to be here."

Five o'clock couldn't come fast enough. Ned and I were ready with our rifles in the racks and ammo in our pack; there's no way you can keep us in the sack.

Mona had omelets, toast, and coffee for breakfast; and we are out the door. Ned and Gerald went across the lake and headed up Waltons mountain while Mick, Tony, and I headed for the phone booth. The wind was from the southwest and a good breeze at that. Glassing the hills and bogs, we were soon looking at a good bull just outside the tree line in a horseshoe-shaped bog. "Are you ready for a run?" Tony asked. "You bet. But keep it to a walk; my running days have long passed." With that, we were off, headed south. Ten minutes out, Mick called with news of a four point and a cow northwest. "Let's keep going south," I said; and again we were on the move, headed down through the black spruce. And I want to tell you—that shit is nasty; it will grab your boots and drop you on your face in a heartbeat. We were moving at a good clip-covering ground. The whole time, the wind was in our face, off the hill and across the bottoms; then came the dreaded uphill. I began to sweat and breathe hard. Tony kept asking, "Need a break?" "Not yet, keep going." But it wasn't long before I had to shed my shirt. I started to cook. The pace was steady the whole way, 1.21 miles, according to the Global Positioning System; but I got news for you—that's not the way we came.

Mick told Tony where the bull was, and we moved toward that location. Tony glassed the area while I tried to breathe. "There he is," in a whisper. I looked. "Where?" "Right there. Over my finger by the deadwood. See him?" "No." "Just inside the tree line." "No. I guess I'm blind." "There, he's moving. He's maybe a ten point. He's gone." "Let's move up on that bald knob for a better look." "Mick, you on this one," Tony called. "Where is he?" "Can't find him." I remained on watch while Tony looked from different angles, trying to lay his eye on him. No luck. "Let's move to the north of the bog. He's laid up in there; he'll come out." We waited and watched, and Tony would move to the left and then to the right, do a little cow calling to draw him out, but no sign of him. "Mick, you on this one?" "Do you see him?" "No, but he's in there. He hasn't come out." I watched till noon, had a sandwich, and watched some more. Over my shoulder, Tony came running in. "He's up. Come here." And he ran back to his spot. I grabbed my glasses and joined him. "See him?" "Where?" "Just off the point." "No." "There he goes. He's moving up. Mick, you on this one?" "Yeah." "Go east, he's moving up. Get around him." We grabbed our packs and took off, headed east, started swinging south, then west through that nasty shit called black spruce. "Need a break?" "No, keep going." We slowed to a walk. "Mick, you on this one?" "Yeah." "Where is he?" "Just over the spruce, in that small yellow bog." Tony pointed. "In there." I'm thinking to myself that the wind is wrong. "Oh shit," came Mick, "There's a cow straight north of you. She's got your scent." With that, Tony and I climbed on a big rock to get over the spruce. "There he is." The bull went northwest when the cow took off, knowing something was wrong. "I see him." He's moving fast, his back to us and palmated rack, over the spruce. "Wait for a shot." Just sixty yards away, I can't find one. He moves out of sight. "That damn cow got us." "There he is." He's in the open looking for us two hundred yards straight on. "Can you take him, skipper?" I wrapped the sling around my arm, shouldered my rifle, took aim as the sling came tight, took a breath, and tried to steady the crosshairs on his brisket. The bull turned 180 degrees and took off three hundred yards, stopped, and turned broadside. "Can't do it," I said, "too far. I can't hold it steady enough without a rest." We watched as the bull joined the cow and trotted away. "That damn cow," Tony said. "That's why he wouldn't come out, he already had a cow with him. Then he didn't wind us, she did, and away they went. We'll never get close enough to him again today, so let's take a break," I agreed. We found a small rock we could sit on and pulled out a drink. "Mick, you on this one?" No answer. "Mick, you on this one?" No answer again. Tony grabbed his pack and pulled out another radio, turned it on, and we caught the exchange between Mick and Gerald. Small bull and cow, north slope off the lake. "OK. We're on him," Tony said. "Ned's on a small bull." "Let's listen," I said. So we remained on that rock and listened to their talk as Ned and Gerald made their way after the bull. "Next yellow bog." "Move east." "Go slow, you're close." Ned took the point, picking his way, trying ever so hard not to make any noise, working his way around a small point. "There he is. Straight on, sixty-five yards." Ned's crosshairs focused center on his brisket. "You got him." Mick came over the radio. The bull moved about twenty yards and went down in a heap. "He's down," Gerald said. "Well, good job," I told Tony.

We packed back up and headed west to the bogs over the next hill. Mick came on the radio, "I got a bull just bedded in a bog northwest." "Let's go, skipper." And away we went again, moving down off the hill we were on, through the bogs and moving as fast as we could. "Need a break?" "No, keep going." Our pace was steady for about an hour when Tony asked, "Need a drink?" "Yeah, sure," I came back. "Where's the bull?" "OK, skipper, another mile and a half yet." "OK. Let's go!" "Mick, you on this one?" "Yeah, where are you?" Tony explained our location, and Mick's reply was, "Holy shit! I didn't think you'd be that far." So on we pushed farther north over yellow bog after yellow bog. Tony stopped and glasses in front. "Over there," he pointed. I grabbed my glasses and searched. "See the big rock there on the left?" "Yeah." "Now look to the right, another rock." "I got him just over that rock." "Yeah, maybe two." "Right." "We've still got a forty-five-minute push, skipper." "Let's go." And on we went at a bit slower pace. We moved to about 250 yards from the animal still bedded in the yellow bog. Tony and I are lower than the animal and can't see. "You go on alone, skipper." And away I went, moving slow and straight on, keeping low to be undetected by the moose with the wind still in my face. Everything is perfect. Getting closer, I'm walking hunched over and low to the ground. I paused for a moment, looking through the trees, watching the moose flick its ears. "I don't see any horns; the bull must be behind the rock." I went to my knees in the slop and water, knowing I must move to the right to look around the rocks. Crawling on my hands, keeping some black spruce between me and the cow, I moved from a six-o'clock position to a four-o'clock position and still only found one animal. I'm within forty yards, and she has no idea I'm here. She is still in her bed, looking in front of her and smelling what's in back of her. Man, oh man, I should have brought my bow. Tony could have brought her to her feet with the clap of his hands, and I'd be ready to make my shot. *Well, you know, she's right there, and this may be your only chance you better take the shot,* I'm thinking. I raised my 06, wrapped the sling around my left arm, and cradled the rifle tight to my shoulder and clicked off my safety. She's clearly in my scope, looking straight in my direction but still relaxed. In a split second, she looked north, exposing her neck, and my 06 roared. She went over. She attempted to come to her feet as I placed another in her shoulder. All goes still, and my hunt is a success. Tony approached with a "Good shot, skipper. I thought you was gonna give her a kiss; you were so close," remark. "No, I was looking for the bull and couldn't find him; then I was so close I figured I better take her while I had the chance. One in the hand is worth two in the bush, you know." "That's right. And you got some mighty good eatin' there, skipper. Well, I'd better get to work, clean her up today, and we'll pack her out tomorrow. It's too late today." The task of quartering the animal was made to look easy, as Tony worked his knife and laid the animal out to keep the flies away. With work done, we washed our hands in a bog, donned our packs, and headed for camp, which, according to our GPS, was well over a mile away as the crow flies.

The excitement was high in camp that night, as we celebrated over Ned's bull and my cow. Ned told of how he took his bull jumping over a fence at three hundred yards and placed the shot right in his eye to avoid loss of any meat. But I'm not sure about that; I didn't see any fence.

As I sit here at the table in camp, I'm completing a rough draft to this hunt. Waiting for the plane to take us home, happy to go home, and sad to leave the new friends we've made: Mona, a wonderful cook, and Tony, Gerald, and Mick, our guides that work so hard to find us the animals and get us in for a shot and then work ever so hard to get it out. All the meat came out on their backs. Neither Ned nor I carried a pound of the 355 pounds they brought out. And by the way, the weather was warm, almost too warm. It was easy to sweat.

The end has come to another great adventure. I wonder what I'll be doing next.

Chapter 8

BEARS, BEARS, BEARS

It was just after 6:00 PM when a bear appeared just inside the clearing to the left of the bait. It appeared to be very cautious, searching for any movement in the area. Assured it was safe to enter, the bear approached the bait. I was perched in a triple clump of white birch trees just twenty-two yards away, quietly watching and listening to the bear's movements. I could hear no other sound nor see any other movements in the area. The bear picked up a huge bone, threw his head back, and walked back into the heavy cover. *That's a legal bear*, I thought to myself. It's illegal to harvest a sow with this year's cubs. This bear was all alone, and I estimated that the bear's weight was in excess of 225 to 250 pounds. He'll be back.

On previous hunts, I have watched many sows with twin and even triplet cubs enter a baited area. One particular hunt comes to mind when there were two different sows, both with triplet cubs, that fed at the site I was hunting at. One sow walked straight in to the bait and brought her three cubs right in with her. The little guys played around and also fed at the site. The hemlock tree I was in at this site was only fifteen yards away. The little guys were playing and running around, and one cub ran right up my tree, directly under my stand. I looked at the cub and said in a very soft voice, "You can go back to Mom now. I really didn't need her up here too." The cub went back to Mom at the bait without incident, and believe me, I felt much better with him over there and not in my tree. I removed my camera from my day pack, waited, and watched until all three cubs and Mom were at the bait. Moving very slow at all times, I got all four animals in my viewfinder. With automatic flash and automatic wind, I really wasn't sure what would happen when I touched the shutter button. My thoughts were of, *Well here goes.* And it happened: the shutter clicked, the flash went off, and the automatic wind hummed. The adult bear jumped into the air and looked in my direction. I remained completely motionless as the bear looked around, searching to find where it all came from. With everything appearing to be OK, Mom went back to feeding. I decided to take another. This time, all Mom did was turn her head to look and continued feeding. After going through all this, neither picture turned out. This sow and cubs returned one other night for my viewing entertainment. She walked directly to the bait at a fairly quick pace without any hesitation, looked in my direction as much as to say, "Hi, how are you tonight?"

The other sow with triplets acted altogether different. She was very cautious and completely circled the bait—checking for scent, sound, and motion. She didn't bring her cubs in to feed. Instead, she put all three cubs up a tree then very cautiously entered to feed. She didn't remain long, retrieved her cubs, and left the area. With completely different behaviors, I was sure these were different sows, both with triplets.

So this year, I brought my video camera to film such activity. After the bear left the area, I turned on the camera I had on a small platform to the right of my stand, focused it in the area I expected the bear to return to, and started recording. I then retrieved my PSE Fireflite Express from its hook on one of the triple birch trees. My bow is set up to shoot, a 2213 XX75 camo across a long over draw. I'm pulling seventy-two pounds draw weight, which sends my arrows to their intended target at 247 feet per second; at this time in 1989 or '90, it was a very fast and flat arrow. I removed my protective head net completely from my head. This gives me unobstructed view, a lesson I learned when I shot to the left of a bear on a previous hunt. With the net apparently folded in front of my right eye, I sighted on my prey with my left eye, which completely changed the sight picture and caused a complete miss to the left. Needless to say, the bear didn't stick around for a second shot.

I am now ready. I listen to the bear, just inside the cover, breaking the bone apart with his powerful jaws. I remain quiet and motionless for at least forty-five minutes while the bugs eat the shit out of me.

Spring bear hunting in Canada is a great chance to go hunting again in-between fall-to-fall hunts. The only problem is the bugs. On other hunts, I have taped my pants to my boots, my sleeves to my gloves, and almost went crazy with the constant hum of mosquitoes. I remember one spring hunt when I took my girlfriend, Jenifer, with me. She is a very accomplished archer, with two State Style Championships under her belt and success with whitetail hunting. I told her that spring bear hunting was no picnic and that if she could make it through the first night without going completely crazy, she would be all right. Each night before entering her stand, I made sure she was bug proof and had bug dope if she got into trouble. On the fourth night, she said her seat was too low and asked me to fix it. I left the truck and entered the woods and, very quietly, climbed her tree and fixed her seat. When I returned to the ground, she was at the base of the tree. I whispered, "Are you all set?" She nodded her head yes, and I very quietly left the area. I took the truck on to my stand about a half mile away, where I remained in my stand between three and four hours until dark. Upon my return, I found her by the road and ready to enter the safety of the truck. Her face and neck were all bit up. Apparently, she didn't have her head net on correctly and the blackflies had a picnic. She didn't want to use the bug dope because the scent would spook the bears, and they wouldn't enter the baited area. By the next morning, one eye was swelled shut, and her neck was also a mess. She looked like she had been in a fight with a heavyweight champion and lost. But even so, she returned to her stand again the next night to continue her vigil.

With no other bears around, I'm ready to make my shot if this bear returns to the baited area. The time passed slowly as I waited and listened to the bear and other sounds of the woods, a very peaceful way to vacation. There was a movement, south side of the bait. He's checking the area again. He's moving toward the feed broadside, twenty-two yards away. *Remain motionless and wait for an opportunity to move,* are my thoughts. I didn't have to wait long. He turned his back to me. *Perfect.* I come to full draw with completely no noise, my anchor feels good, I drop my fluorescent orange pin to the top of his back, and wait. Again, my waiting period is short when he turns slightly to the south, giving me a good quartering-away shot. I drop the pin midbody behind the ribs to be my point of entry and the arrow to pass through the lung and liver. With pressure to the trigger, the arrow is released and sent to its mark twenty-two yards away at 247 feet per second. The white veins and white knock hit the black fur at precisely the point of my intention. The bear takes the hit with great surprise, makes a quick squat, and dashes for cover. I listen to the sounds of crashing timber and the snapping of limbs under the paws of my swiftly moving prey. But again, not long as the woods again become quiet.

A standard rule we use when hunting bears is not to leave your tree for forty-five minutes after making a shot on a bear because a bear will circle back and make ambush on his own trail. With all quiet, I took a seat and looked at my video camera. The screen is black. *Oh no, the battery went dead,* I thought, *hell.* It all went so perfect; that would have been a real treasure, but as luck would have it, it's lost. I may never have the opportunity again to film a chain of events like the one that just happened.

Time passes slowly, so slowly, waiting to leave the tree to check for sign. I've been on many bear hunts before and trailed many bears into the woods and swamps. Trailed some, it seems for a mile, and the trail just runs out, but every bear we ever harvested we found in less than a hundred yards.

My time has finally lapsed. I drop my bow down to the ground safely on a drop line and climb to the ground. With bow in hand, I move quietly toward the area the bear was in when I shot, a spot easily found by the disturbed earth. My prey only made about two strides before leaving a red trail marker on the ground. Here is where I left my hat. I left the area and went to my truck and waited until time to pick up Steve and Jim, the two fellows I was with on this particular hunt. In the morning, we returned to the area to retrieve my game. I took them directly to the spot where I left my hat and pointed out the trail. It was a good trail, easy to follow, ten yards; here's what is left of your arrow, still an easy trail. Just walk down the bear path and follow the red marks. Fifty yards, seventy-five yards. We better start leaving toilet paper markers to find our way out because it's easy to lose your bearings following a twisted trail back into these swamps. Still a good trail. One hundred yards, one hundred twenty-five. I'm starting to become concerned. I've never found a dispatched bear this far from the shot. The trail leads on and goes through some tight areas and always on the level, never climbing, which we felt was a good sign. Then it happened; all sign stopped. We circled the area, looked for sign on my hands and knees, and nothing. We looked for about an hour, nothing. We estimated we followed the trail about a half mile with an unsettling conclusion, no bear. In reviewing the shot in my mind, I feel the bear must have been standing more broadside than I thought, and the arrow passed behind the vitals instead of entering under the rib cage and up into the chest. We did all we could but were unsuccessful in locating this bear. As I said before, I have never found a bear that went more than a hundred yards after the shot. The hit just wasn't good enough.

On this particulate hunt, Jim harvested a bear and Steve passed on a couple of small bears. It's great to be with friends and experience the great outdoors, with its trials and tribulations. As for myself, next time, two batteries, maybe three—whatever it takes.

Chapter 9

FIVE PONDS

Wilderness, my kind of country. An area set aside never to be developed, to be wild for generations to come.

While on a recent canoe trip, brother-in-law Keith and I made tentative plans for Columbus Day weekend, a three-day weekend in October. If the weather is bad, he'll help Jenny and I on our studio. If the weather is good, we'll go for a walk. As the date grew closer, I watched the weather forecast for an indication of what I should plan. It appeared there would be a little rain Friday night, then clear the rest of the weekend. I called Keith, and we decided a backpack trip would fill the order just fine. "Meet me in Wannakenna, 9:00 AM, Saturday morning," I said, "and plan for three days, two nights, and twenty-plus miles." He agreed and I began to pack.

This will be a test run. What do I need and don't need should I attempt the AT (Appalachian Trail)? As I said before, I have no intention of tackling the whole trail, but I would like to experience some of it. Also, I want to test new equipment. Jaime has been pushing the internal frame pack, a hammock to sleep in, and I'm sure Keith and I will have other options to discuss.

Jenny and I packed two dinners, eggs for breakfast, and peanut-butter sandwiches for lunch, and trail mix to snack on. Also, my water purifier and coffee to drink. Sweats to sleep in, shirt, T-shirt, jeans, a jacket, water bottle, flashlight, compass, GPS, and my pocket digital camera. Oh yeah, a sleeping bag too. All packed up and only twenty-two pounds. Not bad. Keith was going to bring a pack stove, and I have the water purifier. There is no need to have two.

Unable to sleep Saturday morning, I left the house at 5:30 AM. Wannakenna is only an hour and a half away. I'll make a quick stop for breakfast and still arrive early. Maybe I'll take a nap. When I pulled into

Wannakenna, there was a deer target close to the road. *That's an odd place for a target,* I thought. So I backed up. Its ear moved; then its head turned my way. I reached for my camera, put my window down, and took a picture. She turned and started walking toward me. She has been fed, I'm sure and looking for a handout. "Sorry, girl, I don't have anything for you today."

In need of another cup of coffee, I drove into Wannakenna village, but nothing was open. The general store doesn't open until 9:00 AM. There is a restaurant on the road to the Ranger School, but it too was not open. A lady walking her dog told me, "Your best bet is Cranberry Lake." "Oh well, I guess I really don't need it."

Wannakenna is an old logging town. Loggers lived in town and walked across a footbridge to the mill. The bridge still stands and is now listed on the National Register of Historic Places. It spans the Oswegatchie River as proudly today as it did over a hundred years ago.

In the center of town, a three-sided billboard tells the history of Wannakenna. Pictures and captions give you a clear picture of what life was like here as a logging town.

Keith and Clancy arrived at 9:00 AM. The store opened, I grabbed a bottle of water, and we drove to the trailhead. A quick sign in, throw on your backpack, and we're off. Our itinerary takes us down an old railroad bed to the end of Dead Creek Flow, a real easy walk. It's all flat, you won't find a better trail than this one. At the end of the railroad bed, the trail turns to a more primitive state, although we did cross several wooden bridges before the junction to Janacks Landing. Another sign in, and the trail gets rougher; bridges are now just logs to walk on.

The fall is a beautiful time to go for a walk. Your visual adventure is enhanced by the aromas that fill the air—balsam fir, autumn leaves, and the smell of fresh clean air. This area is the Five Ponds Wilderness. I don't believe any logging has been done here in about one hundred years. As we walked, we saw cherry trees twenty and twenty-two inches across and straight as an arrow. Giant birch, maple, and pine as big as forty-two inches across. These are visions you won't find just anywhere.

At the junction for High Falls, we turn west and head down a draw into marsh country. An area of devastation from a microburst I believe came through around '95. In places, it looked like Paul Bunyan dropped a whole box of matchsticks we call trees and were left where they lay because this is wilderness. We found carvings in log butts dating '98, which gives you an indication how long it took to reopen this trail.

In this lower marsh area, we crossed a beaver dam that had to be six feet high and thirty yards across. Also several small log bridges and one single bridge at least sixty feet long. And believe me, slippery when wet. No, I didn't fall in.

We arrived at the junction of High Falls and the primitive corridor, which takes you back to Wannakenna, 8.6 miles, and again I believe to be an old railroad bed. Our destination, High Falls, is a short 0.4 miles away. On this section of trail, we found an old log skidder that is resting, I'm sure, where it made its final skid. Just another bit of history.

Our lean-to was empty and ours for the night. My first job was to make myself a cup of coffee and take a short break. Keith and I caught up on everything that had happened since Labor Day. Then we gathered firewood, filtered water, and explored the area. I crossed the river at the head of the falls and found the west lean-to just as a man was putting down his canoe paddles. I was in awe of his accomplishment; he had paddled eighteen miles upstream in six hours alone. A man about my age, I was impressed.

The cement abutments are still here that supported another footbridge. In 1963, I walked from Wannakenna to High Falls, and I can't remember if I saw the bridge or not. I may have just seen a picture of it; I'm really not sure.

While gathering firewood, Keith and I were unable to locate the trail to Nicks Pond and Cowhorn Junction. This was to be our route to Cat Mountain on day 2. Apparently, it was never reopened after the microburst.

Evening was short. It got dark shortly after 7:00 PM. Keith had an inflatable seat with a back support he used while sitting around the campfire, and later I used it for a mattress to sleep on over the wooden floor and found it to be very comfortable. Keith also brought a hammock he hung inside the lean-to. The idea is that it keeps you off the ground making for less chance of hypothermia. In the morning, Keith claimed a good night's sleep, not at all uncomfortable. I too slept well. My only complaint was my head got cold. A tuke would have been nice. Clancy was shivering, so apparently he got cold. He could have slept on my head or just curled up with me. I wouldn't have minded the extra heat; wouldn't mind it at all.

Morning dawned, a beautiful day; *not* it rained in the night, and there was still a mist in the air. After breakfast, we packed up and headed for Cat Mountain, only four and a half miles away. Ponchos are a must in this type of weather and make it large enough to cover your backpack as well. I also put my sleeping bag in a plastic bag then put it in my stuff sack. You can believe me when I say, "A wet bag is no fun, no fun at all."

Walking down the trail, it wasn't long, and my jeans were wet, and they were still wet twenty-five hours later when I arrived at my truck. Keith wore nylon pants, and they dried in an hour. Remember that for the next time.

Cat Mountain has a beautiful overlook and not a bad climb either. Below lies Cat Mountain Pond; to the south, Three Mile Mountain; and to the north, Glasby Pond and Dead Creek Flow. Fall colors are on, although the reds are mostly on the ground. The yellow, orange, and green still make a colorful tapestry. We encountered four other groups near Cat Mountain; I really didn't think we'd find anyone up here.

We left Cat Mountain and headed for Janacks Landing, about two and a half miles away. Janacks Landing is named for the man that manned the fire tower on Cat Mountain. A logging accident left him with only one leg. Consequently, his logging career was over. Mr. Janack's cabin was at the head of Dead Creek Flow. In the summertime, he would walk the eight-hundred-foot climb over two and a half miles of trail almost every day on one leg.

When we arrived at Janacks Landing, again the lean-to was ours to use, and again I needed a cup of coffee. We settled in, gathered firewood for what we expected to be a cold night. We started the fire early to dry out my jeans and boots. As I said, Keith dried out in an hour; nylon, remember that. Before bed, Keith stoked the fire well, and there was still a bed of coals in the morning. It took little effort to rekindle a fire and soak up the much-needed heat.

When breakfast was over, we packed up our gear, put out the fire, and headed for our trucks about three miles away. Again an easy walk, and too soon it was over.

If you're interested in a look back in time, Wannakenna may be what you're looking for, and Cat Mountain would be an easy-day hike. Check it out. I'm sure you won't be disappointed.

Chapter 10

SUMMER OF '04

September 10. Where has the summer gone? Jenny and I are putting an addition on our home to use as a photography studio and gallery. It is my intention to retire from the carpenter work and put my energy in a different direction. I'm too young to stop working altogether, but carpentry work is hard on my body. After forty years of it, I'll make a career change while I still can. The summer has, to say the least, been busy; work all week on the job and all weekend at home. *But* we did manage to load the canoe on the truck for the Fourth of July and Labor Day. It was great to get away.

July found us putting our canoe in at the dam of lower St. Regis Lake. Our destination is Upper St. Regis lean-to, a spot we camped about fifteen years ago. On board this time were Kevin and Diane, and Diane's friend, Sherry. Sherry boarded her canoe alone and would try to keep a forward movement with almost no experience. I offered to take it for her and she declined. She wanted to try, and try she did until Spitfire, when the waves were so big there was only fear. Fear of capsizing, fear of drowning, and most of all, the fear of losing her *beer*! Man, I'm glad I don't drink that stuff. It weighs eight pounds to every gallon. I'll take my water purifier and instant coffee, thank you. Well, where was I? Back on Spitfire, Sherry was pretty well exhausted and didn't object one bit to me taking over for her. At Rabbit Island, I slid out of my canoe and into hers. She seemed relieved. It was less gear and my sweetheart Jenny to help paddle. I pushed offshore, pointed her canoe toward Upper St. Regis, and took the lead. When I left the channel between Spitfire and Upper St. Regis, I turned northwest, and Jenny said she never saw me again until they arrived at camp. Guess I'm not dead yet, huh.

We settled in, gathered firewood and relaxed around the campfire. Me with my coffee, Jenny and Kevin with ice tea, and Diane and Sherry with a beer; and I know I heard someone say, "Man this is great." My feelings exactly.

Day 2. I have St. Regis Mountain in my sights, anyone else? Jenny and I plan to have lunch at the top. As I donned my day pack, the rest were ready to go. A short hike to the base of the mountain and a sign in gives us the feeling—*we're not alone.* Several parties have already headed up, and it's only 10:00. If my memory serves me well, this is a strenuous climb, 3.3 miles according to the sign in.

I felt we were maybe halfway when Diane began to shake. She hadn't been feeling right that summer and couldn't go up any farther, so she headed back for camp. Jenny and I continued across a bolder field called a trail, and I must comment on the work done by the college students. Stone steps were laid by hand to make a stairway in several spots. Nice job, but still a real climb in elevation.

We reached the top at about 1:30, and the view was just as I remembered it, breathtaking in all directions. In the distance, Whiteface and Algonquin and farther south, Mt. Marcy, and at our feet lay Upper St. Regis, Spitfire, and Lower St. Regis, south to the seven and nine carries and upper Saranac. Pristine, plush green forest land, sparkling waterways, and blue skies. What more could there possibly be? With Jenny right here beside me, it just doesn't get any better than this.

The fire tower remains standing but a little rough, I might add. It hasn't seen any repair in a few years but still stands and acts as a beacon to all travelers in the area, an excellent reference point. If you can see the tower, you know where you are and should know which way to go, unless you think the Martians moved it because it's on the wrong mountain. "Jerk," as my wife would say.

Travel was slow on the way down. Jenny twisted her ankle, and my knees were bothering me. As people passed, they almost all commented, "It's sure easier going down than up." But I'm not sure about that.

Day 3. I would like to check out the St. Regis canoe area. All wilderness, no motors, or mechanical devices such as wheels for your canoe to aid your portage. This is my kind of country. I love my peace and quiet. Jenny said, "No." Her ankle hurts; Kevin wanted to fish. Sherry wanted to read and relax. Diane said, "I'll go." And away we went. The portage from Upper St. Regis to Bog Pond was short and easy and someone had laid up a beautiful stonewall here. Also on this portage, I met a man in a beautiful wooden canoe. I believe he said it was like George Sears's canoe, Little Paddler, only this one is three pounds lighter than his, a mere seventeen pounds. Fascinating. Then, on to Bear Pond, a point by the pond is now the home of a lean-to. Fifteen years ago, I saw a bright yellow tent here from the mountaintop. Then over into Little Long Pond, where we visited with a man and his dog who have camped here every July 4 for five years. "Just me and my dog," he said. Then over to Green Pond and St. Regis Pond, where a pair of loons chattered their warning of intruders. At least that's what I call it, and I'm sure no authority so take that for what it's worth.

All the portages were well marked, and campsites were easy to find. I'll be back someday, and maybe I'll stay a day or two.

Diane and I turned our canoe around and headed back to camp. In the Upper St. Regis Lake, we again marveled at what has been called the Great Camps. Our canoe silently slipped by some of the most beautiful estates you will ever find anywhere, and Upper St. Regis Lake is home to an abundance of them. Our quiet campfire gave way to a fantastic fireworks display right in front of our site. A marvelous Fourth of July celebration and definitely a time to reflect on our troops on foreign soil.

Day 4. Packing up and headed home. Our paddle out was completed in just two hours. Not bad, not bad at all.

After killing myself all summer, working the job and trying to make progress on our studio, Labor Day was a welcome sight. Again, we elected to take four days. This time, Keith and Jaime would meet us at Racket Lake village, unload our gear, and then shuttle a truck to Long Lake, our destination. Jenny and I arrived at Racket Lake village at 10:50, unloaded, and waited an hour and a half for Keith and Jaime. At 12:30, Keith drove by, turned around, and headed out. He never looked our way, so I yelled, "HEY!" His head snapped our way, and he stopped. "What are you doing here?" he said. "Waiting for you!" "Well, Jaime and I were waiting for you at the Golden Beach State Park. I just came to get a soda." Don't ask me where the mix-up occurred; I have no idea. Jenny said next time Jaime and I will set it up, "Jerk."

By the time we shuttled the truck, we managed to be on the water by two o'clock. No problem, we're only going to Clark's point today, maybe two miles max. Guess again, Clark's Point is full, no vacancies. What now, Ter? There are more lean-tos at the other end, but we'll have to cross the lake, and I'll bet she's rough. Our only other experiences on Racket were twelve to fourteen inches waves. We paddled alongside Indian Point to its end, slipped over to Birch Point, then headed for Bluff Point straight across. Don't stop paddling here as the waves continue to build. *SPLASH!* "OH SHIT." That one broke inside our canoe. *SPLASH!* It did it again! I knew there was a reason we packed everything in a dry bag. And the book said, "Cross Racket in the morning." Well, that was our plan. Once we slid around Bluff Point, everything calmed down. We passed an empty campsite on Beecher Island. "If Boucher Point is full, we'll come back here." There were three lean-tos at Boucher Point, and they were all empty. Luck was on our side. The moon was full, coming up over the hills. It glistened over the waters of the northeast end of Racket Lake. Peaceful, to say the least.

Day 2. I rose early to watch the sunrise, which really sucked; and worse yet, I didn't want to wake anyone else up, so I didn't even have my coffee. What kind of deal is that? Believe it or not, I did survive. After breakfast, we packed up, and we made ready for our first portage to Forked Lake, a short hop, maybe half a mile. When our canoes hit shore, our life jackets were buckled to the two seats, and the paddles are bungeed to the yoke and front seat. Jenny takes the backpack; and I take the dry bag, hoist the canoe to my shoulders, and we're off. Keith and Jaime have a similar routine. One trip, and we're done. Clancy—that's Keith and Jaime's dog—even has saddlebags for his food. When he has it on, he holds his head high and prances down the trail—proud, real proud. Sadie, our dog, is thirteen years old now. We'll carry her food. We're just glad she's still able to go with us. At the Forked Lake boat launch, another canoe was loaded and ready to push off. The gear in that canoe, I swear, was two feet over the gunnels. I couldn't help myself. I said, "Holy shit, you going for the rest of the summer"? He replied, "You ever been up here when the weather changed?" "It can't change that much! Which way are you headed?" He points to the left. We're going to the right. "Well, enjoy," I said; and we slipped our canoe into the water. As we slid down the lake, there was no one else in sight, just us, not a soul anywhere. We arrived at the only lean-to on the lake, about noon, made camp, then headed for a swim. The water was just a little brisk, not quite hot tub material, if you know what I mean. At bedtime, the breeze was directly at the lean-to from the fire, and it filled our shelter with smoke. Jenny stayed up to read. When I looked in her direction, I couldn't see her. "Jenny, where are you? Give me a knife. I want to cut through the smoke to find you." And she laughed!

Morning dawned to find the girls on the ground. They just couldn't handle the smoke. After breakfast, we packed up and headed for the dam and found people everywhere, camped all along both shores. "It's a campground!" Forked Lake State Campground; the only access to your site is with a boat or canoe. "Neat, real neat." We talked with the ranger in the office. "The water is about a foot higher than normal," he said. "It rained every weekend all summer, and this is our best weekend this season." We packed up to make our longest portage, according to the sign, one and one-third miles to the Pine Brook Lean-to. Jenny has had trouble with her back this summer, and it concerns me. She insists she can carry her share. "If you can't," I said, "just put it down, and I will come back for it." Jaime stepped on a landscape spike this summer, and it got infected, then required surgery to clean it up so it would heal. Both girls did their share and probably more and didn't ever complain.

Back on the water, we paddled to Buttermilk Falls. My map says "*Caution.*" I guess, if you go over that, they'll send you home in a body bag if they find all the pieces. A short stop, a few pictures, then make a real short carry around the falls. It's just a short paddle to our next carry and the worst of our trip. This carry was rugged and, we all agreed, longer than we figured. It took us to our last campsite at the head of Long Lake. The first leant-to was taken, but the next was empty. We made camp, took a swim to refresh ourselves, and then went exploring. I wanted to check out Owls Head Falls. We paddled through a marsh over two beaver dams, one of which was a foot under our canoe, and upstream to the base of the falls. Here, the water is running over a huge—and I mean *huge*—rock at the top and rolls down into a rock-covered stream. On a normal year, it would probably be dry, but don't quote me on that because I'm not sure. I thought it was worth the time to check it out. Compared it to Buttermilk Falls, and it's a disappointment; so don't compare it, and you won't be disappointed.

At three o'clock in the morning, Sadie began to cough and woke me up. She slipped out of the lean-to and wandered around, coughing. I got up to relieve myself and sat down on the lean-to and waited for her return. As I said, she's old, and I need to help her up. Keith got up and also went to the outhouse. When he returned, I said, "Did you see the old brown dog up there?" "No." "Well, where the hell did she go?" We returned with flashlights looking for her with no luck. Then I noticed flashlights in the next lean-to. *OH SHIT, I hope they don't have a gun,* I thought as I trotted the path to their camp. "Hello," I said. "Yea." "You got an old brown dog over here?" I could hear the relief in his voice. "Yea, I'm sure they thought they had a bear wandering around." "Sorry for the intrusion," I said. "Come on, old dog." And we wandered back to bed.

Day 4. We packed up for the last time and headed for Long Lake Boat Launch. Shortly after our departure from shore, Keith spotted a nice black bear wandering the opposite shore. *A real sharp clean animal just wandering, looking for grubs and fish,* I assume. Farther down, we noticed a huge nest in a big pine tree. We assumed it to be an eagle's nest but, again, don't quote me on that one either. All too soon, the bridge is in sight, and our wonderful trip is over. The best of weather, some of the greatest scenery, and the best of company make for a wonderful, wonderful trip.

Chapter 11

LOWES LAKE

Wild, rugged, harsh, difficult, and untamed. These are just a few adjectives I used to describe the wilderness trip I just took.

On Columbus Day weekend '05, I took a trip I had dreamed of since 1987. Several times I'd made plans but just never managed to make the trip, including Labor Day this year. Again I planned, and again it fell through. So when brother-in-law Keith and I were talking about what to do on Columbus Day weekend, he thought the Lowes Lake trip sounded fun. Paddle up the Bog River then across Lowes Lake. Portage over to the headwaters of the Oswegatchie. Then paddle downriver to Inlet. I was excited, to say the least.

In 1987, Jenny, Steph, our two dogs, Mandy and Sadie, and myself took a three-day weekend to explore the area. We found an abundance of campsites around the lake, which has the largest concentration of loons in the north country, I might add. The trail from Lowes Lake to Big Deer Pond was well-worn and easy to walk. I portaged our canoe over the trail and then paddled across the pond. At the end of the pond, we left our canoe and walked the remaining 2.2 miles to the Oswegatchie. It was a beautiful trail through a pristine forest to a campsite at the water's edge. The trail was mostly flat with just one hill. On the hill was a horizontal pole to rest your canoe on and a bench to rest your butt on, a nice spot to take a much-needed break. The remaining trail was mostly a slight downhill walk to the campsite in a stand of pine.

After that weekend in '87, I dreamed of completing this trip, and now it looks like it might actually happen.

The weather has been in the high seventies prior to Columbus Day. But a change is coming. A cold front from the west, dumping snow in Minnesota, and tropical storm Tammy coming up the east coast, dumping several inches of rain in her wake, gave us some concern. Cooler temperatures and light rain were what we were looking at for the weekend. So we loaded my aluminum canoe on Keith's truck along with our other gear, grabbed grandson Owen, and headed for Harrisville—where it has become tradition to stop at a great little diner for breakfast. Then on to Inlet or the Oswegatchie canoe area, whichever you prefer, where we left my truck at the take out. Then a fifty-two-mile road trip through Cranberry Lake, to Tupper Lake, turn right onto Rt. 30 and head south. Next, you see a sign for Horseshoe Lake. Turn right, follow this road to the Bog River area sign, turn left, drive three-fourths mile, and you're there.

On Labor Day this year, we launched here and were quickly hit by a headwind. A wind we battled all the way to Lowes Lake, which slammed us with two-foot waves. It was a real battle to keep a forward movement.

Saturday morning began with cool temperatures and a moderate wind, which appeared to be at our back as we pushed off from the lower dam. Slipping through the channel of the Bog River, you soon realize you're in wilderness. There are no cottages, no motors, and, at this time of year, very few people. The channel began to open up to a larger body of water. We passed under an old railroad bridge, and Keith spotted our national symbol perched in a small pine at the water's edge—a proud, beautiful bald eagle. He watched as we slid by him at just twenty yards. This was Owen's first-ever look at this amazing bird. He experienced it not in a zoo, theme park, or state fair. No, he saw it here in its true habitat, the wild.

We then paddled on into Henchens Pond, and the wind was still at our backs. We landed on a small beach near the grounds, where Lowes homestead once stood. Stonewalls and a stone fireplace remain where the house once stood. The brass grave markers in the pet cemetery are gone, but the impressions remain. A new upper dam was constructed in '93 to replace the old deteriorating one and controls the water level in Lowes Lake. If I remember right, Mr. Lowe also used the dam to generate electricity to power his home. But don't quote me on that one. It was in '87 when I heard that one. Also in '87, the house and other outbuildings were still standing. All that remains now are the stone foundations.

The portage here is short, maybe three hundred yards max. Owen was showing a real interest in the waterfall as we walked over the dam. A short pause and we moved on. We boarded our canoe and paddled on up the Bog River, heading for the lake.

Just before the Boy Scout camp, we headed our canoe out of the main channel and through a marsh section I have never traveled before. This channel never appeared on any of my older maps. It does appear on my new Adirondack Paddlers Map. This channel has a more direct route straight into the lake.

As Keith and I paddled, Owen kept the map on his lap, looking for the next campsite. He seldom missed one. I pointed to campsite 13 with not so fond a memory. On our Labor Day trip here, we were hoping to stop here for the night. Our canoe was hit broadside by two waves, dumping four inches of water into our boat. Not a pretty sight.

Luck was truly on our side today. The wind, still at our backs, pushed us as we passed several loons fishing in the lake.

To my knowledge, there is only one camp on the lake, and it was here that we spotted our second bald eagle. We were not as fortunate this time. He appeared to be a little more skittish than the previous one. He didn't allow us to get as close before he took to the air.

So far, we have only encountered two canoes and one kayak on the water and a couple more on shore. Labor Day was a much different story. There seemed to be people everywhere.

We kept pushing toward the end of the lake. We only have three days to complete this trip. Owen has school, and Keith has a job. Myself, I'm retired; every day is a holiday.

We beached our canoe at campsite 34, made camp, built a fire, and prepared dinner. Our evening was cut short about six o'clock when it began to rain. As I lay in my tent with Owen, we were serenaded by a pair of loons chattering back and forth. Keith and I were sure they would be gone by this time.

Sunday morning, the wind died down, and the rain ended. We had our breakfast, packed up our camp, loaded our canoe, and paddled to the trail head, a short half-mile paddle. Here we donned our packs and prepared for our seven-tenths-of-a-mile hike to Big Deer Pond. This landing is not the way I remember it. My first impression is that it has been moved from the spot I remember from '87. It was brought to my attention that this is correct. Because of the microburst, it has been moved.

We made the portage to the pond with no problem and paddled across. We were greeted on the other side by a sign that reads, "Down trees may impede travel." It was soon apparent that the microburst of '95 had taken its toll. The beautiful trail I remembered was gone. The pristine forest had given away to new growth and underbrush. Some of the trees across the trail had short sections cut out, but that was all. In places, the trail was completely grown over. At the halfway point, the bench has rotted into the ground, and the horizontal pole to rest your canoe on is no longer there. We continued on, ducking under and stepping over downed trees. It seemed to be a very long 2.2 miles. Something new on the trail was a mailbox with the flag up. Inside were notes from earlier travelers about their trip.

Owen, six at this time, completed the hike carrying his own backpack, the boat cushion he used to sit on in the boat, and his life jacket—a real tough little guy and a real joy to be around. We completed out portage by 2:30 PM, just five hours for the entire three and a half miles.

Thinking our work was over, we boarded our canoe and shoved off for the three-mile paddle to High Falls. The river appeared to be high from all the rain of late. With a good current helping us along, we twisted our way downstream until we encountered the first of many logs across the river. The only way through was over. Owen climbed on the log at one end while Keith and I pulled the canoe up and over the log and back into the water. Reboard and paddle to the next.

We passed over several beaver dams. Some completely underwater, others dropped us about a foot as we built up speed and shot over them.

In the distance, we could hear the roar from High Falls, as millions of gallons of water made the plunge to the bottom, churning the water into a white foam. Here, we made a short portage around the falls and paddled across the river to the west lean-to. We took a short break and paused for pictures before making camp.

Much of our gear was still damp from Saturday night. While Owen gathered firewood, Keith and I hung up sleeping bags and other clothing to dry. Here, our evening was much more enjoyable than our previous one—cooking hot dogs over the open fire, me with my coffee, Owen with his hot chocolate, and Keith with his hot tea.

Soon Owen, all on his own, got on his night clothes and climbed into his sleeping bag. It wasn't long, and he was asleep. A rough day for the little guy. I'm sure he's tired.

Morning dawned, another cloudy day. Owen, the first to stir, wanted his scrambled eggs. "And don't forget my pop tart, Grandpa." We packed our gear, took one last look at the falls, and headed downstream to my truck, a twisting eighteen miles away.

A couple more logjams to cross, a footbridge to duck under that I don't remember, and one new lean-to that I'm sure wasn't there before, along with a good look at the devastation from the microburst of '95. In some areas, hardly a tree was left standing. Millions of board feet of lumber were lying on the ground. How long will it take to return to the plush green forest I remember? If I were to venture a guess, I would say about fifty years. Right now, the new growth consists of evergreens and brush. I would truly like to see the area from the air to get an even better look at the destruction Mother Nature has caused. For now, I can only tell you what I see from the ground.

On our voyage out, we only encountered two other groups. They paddled up from Inlet, which I'm sure was no easy task. In most places, we saw no shore; the water disappeared into the brush on both sides.

The sighting of my truck meant the end of our weekend. The end of a trip, I've wanted to take for almost twenty years, a trip your average outdoor adventurer would not call enjoyable. I believe this trip to be much harder now than it was twenty years ago and not because I'm older but because of the devastation Mother Nature has caused. Wilderness does not describe what we encountered; primitive is a much better word in my book.

So if you think you're up for about a twelve-mile paddle through open lake where the wind can blow in any direction, a three-and-a-half-mile portage over a rough trail of blowdowns and under growth, and a twisting twenty-one-mile downstream trip over beaver dams and logjams and boulders. give Lowes Lake to headwaters of the Oswegatchie to Inlet a try. I can guarantee that if you stay away from peak season, you'll stay away from people.

Chapter 12

HOWLAND'S ISLAND

Howland's Island is a 3,300-acre piece of real estate near Weedsport, New York. The island, owned by the state of New York, has about 150 tillable acres. When planted, it provides a crop of usually corn to all who reside there and deer, turkeys, waterfowls, and upland birds as well.

The first time I went hunting on the island was a controlled hunt, one day a year, and bow hunters only. We arrived near the island with a camper trailer the night before the hunt and made camp. The cars, trucks, and campers came in all night long and most of the next morning. You were not allowed to scout or get any head start at all. The gate was opened at 6:00AM, and the invasion began. I don't believe I've ever seen so many hunters in one place before. I had never been on the island prior, so it was all new to me and my hunting companions. We wandered most of the morning, stopping now and then and watched for a while. After lunch, I found some swale grass and cattails next to a dike. I left my friends on the dike and drove the cattails, hoping for some action for my friends, and action they got. The deer came out all over the dike and avoided my friends, so I went in again and again. Every time I went in, the deer came out. The only problem was when they came out, they were usually on the run and a little hard to hit with a bow. We were unsuccessful on our first visit to the island, but I was sure I would be back.

Jen and I spent many days on the island in the years that followed. The island became open for the entire season the next year following my first visit. Every weekend during bow season found us putting up stands and enjoying the area. One weekend morning found me on the island with Jim, my cousin, setting on my watch before daylight. I can see the image of a deer coming down the trail. With not enough shooting light, I had no choice but to let the deer pass. As the time passed, my watch was uneventful till a nice eight point came into view. He was on the trail leading directly by my watch. On this day, I was on the ground, sitting in front of a bush to break up my outline. Short of my watch, the buck turned and headed up the hill. With this turn, my bow came swiftly up and to full draw. I hit my anchor perfectly and concentrated on the buck and my pin. My target was within twenty yards and moving uphill. He's behind a tree, now a bush, and still moving. No shot, be patient. With all my concentration on the buck, the weight of the bow seemed to be nothing. The buck is now on the same level as I am. He's turned and heading straight for me, his nose on the ground and my sight pin on his head. No shot here, be patient. My heart is pounding as I wait for an opening, an opportunity to put the arrow in the right spot. The buck continues toward me in a straight line—fifteen yards, ten, and now only five yards form the tip of my arrow. His ears snap forward, and he's motionless in his tracks. Panic hits his eyes. My heart pounds. The sight pin still on his head, I remained rigid in my stance, waiting. The buck jerked his head up and to his right, my pin found a spot on his neck, and without another thought, the arrow was on its way. With only feet to travel, the arrow met its mark in a split second; the impact knocked the buck right off this feet. I quickly jumped to mine and grabbed another arrow while the buck thrashed in an attempt to get back on his feet. I loaded, drew, and planted another arrow deep into the buck's chest. Seconds later, the thrashing stopped, and the buck was mine. Not exactly a textbook take by any means, but other than a bear cub under my stand, I have never been this close to a game animal before. My heart pounded from the adrenaline rush; the complete sequence couldn't have taken three minutes, and this is hunting at its best.

About two years after this, Jenny joined me for a three-day hunt on the island. It was the last weekend of bow hunting before the regular season opened. We moved our stands a couple of times, trying to get closer to the deer passing us. Always just out of bow range. On the last day, Jenny had two deer directly under her stand in the morning but was unable to get a shot. That evening it all came together for her. A doe again walked directly under her stand and continued to feed. With daylight fading fast, she made her shot. The deer bolted, crashing through the woods; then all went quiet. She called me on the radio for assistance. I arrived to find a trail, easy to follow that led me directly to a fine doe just thirty-five yards away. With excitement, she told me how her light was fading, and the deer remained too close to her for a clean shot. She knew it was now or never. It was nearly a straight-down shot and, as most bow hunters know, one of the most difficult. Luck was in her corner, and the arrow found its mark.

One of the tales I love to tell of Howland's Island also happened on the final day of bow season. My friend Bill, Jenny, and I again had moved our stands, trying to get a shot at a nice buck. Again, always too far away. On this day, it was pouring down rain, I mean pouring. I noticed a deer coming from Bill's area. It's the buck. He's on the trail that will pass me just twenty yards out. The buck moved behind a tree just as I came to full draw. His vitals are blocked by the tree allowing me no shot. *Shit. Just one step, come on, just one.* He was at the ridge behind the tree, then one bound, and he was gone. "Shoot, darn, poop," as I always say; that's it the buck is gone bow season is over. So I removed my stand from the tree and returned my equipment to the truck. I climbed to the ridge to get Jenny and her equipment. Walking along the ridge, I kept looking for Jenny. I knew she was here somewhere. Then I spotted her. She was on the ground with her bow in her hand, looking away. I stopped and remained still, trying to see what she was looking at. She placed her bow on the ground and put her hands in her pockets. I began my descent down off the ridge toward her. I got within ten yards of her, and she didn't even know I was coming so now I'm quiet. I got within four inches of her ear, and I snorted. She went about four feet straight up. When she came down, she called me everything but honey. "You son of a bitch, you just took ten years off my life." We picked up her equipment and laughed all the way to the truck.

    I don't have paper enough to tell all the tales I have of Howland's Island. It's truly a great place to hunt or just go for a walk. If you're ever around Weedsport, New York, check it out. It may just be the beginning of some great memories for you.

Chapter 13

HUDSON RIVER

I have taken many trips on the Hudson from Newcome to North Creek, a section of river known as the white water of New York. My first trip, a friend asked if my partner, Eric, and I would be interested in running this section of the river. He had no experience running white water and wanted us to go along because Eric had the experience and some river savvy. We agreed to go. Eric had a four-man raft he would use. I chose to build one—just an intertube sandwiched between two pieces of plywood. The river was low this time of year, so I just wanted to protect my tube from rock damage and gently drift down the river. The idea worked just fine, except I didn't have any place for my sleeping bag, so I threw my bag into Eric's raft. The first rough section of river was long falls, navigable in times of the year when there is more water but certainly not today. I had to walk my tube through the jungle of rock. On our way through, we saw remains of others who had come before us. Rafts, canoes, and kayaks broken in half or bent around a rock. "Wow, look at that, man. This river can take its toll." I think a man could get killed in here in the spring. So we continued on down the river, paddling when we could and walking the rest of the time. By the end of the day, we were tired. I pulled up on a neat point, a real great campsite, and helped the other guys with their gear. When I grabbed my sleeping bag, I swear it weighed 150 pounds. Eric's did too. I threw them onto a rock and kneeled on them to wring out as much water as I could. Oh boy, this is going to be fun. In order to sleep in this, I must dry it out. We gathered firewood and had a bonfire about six feet high, had our bags on two horizontal poles, and continued to turn them over. After a bite to eat and a check on the map, we determined there wasn't enough time to make the entire trip. The water was just too slow. So an escape plan was in the works. We located a woods road down river about a mile. That's our way out tomorrow.

Eric couldn't hold his head up, so he grabbed his bag and went to bed. Ray, Bob, and I sat around the fire with coffee and good conversation for a while until they turned in as well. I, on the other hand, stayed with the fire until it was all but out. Snug in my nice damp bag, I hadn't been asleep long when all of a sudden the fire exploded back to flames about two feet high. I immediately jumped to my knees, rubbed my eyes, and saw Eric on the other side with his sleeping bag over his head and everything within arm's length on that fire. He was freezing right to death and had to get warm.

That was our first crack at the famed Hudson River, but we are not finished. We'll try again next year during the spring run off.

The next year found us looking at a much wilder river on Memorial Day weekend. This time, the four of us were taking our chances in inflatable kayaks. On the river from Newcome again and headed downstream, making good time. The kayaks skimmed over the water with little effort, and my gear was securely wrapped in plastic bags to hopefully ensure a dry dreamland tonight.

Our first obstacle would be long falls, a roaring hellhole of rock and raging white water. We were spaced apart about a hundred yards when we rounded the corner, and there they were. *Holy shit, grab your life jacket and get it on*; and in I went, my kayak diving in and out of sight. At times, the water came up to my chest. My thoughts were, "Just keep her straight, don't go broadside and roll her over." My heart pounded with the adrenaline rush; the kayak paddle cutting the water on whichever side needed to keep her straight. I looked up quickly to see nothing, just white. *Keep paddling.* I'm in a fight for my life; the power of this water is astronomical. Separation from my kayak could prove deadly. I completed long falls without a catch, thank God. In the eddy at the end, I again joined my friends in cheers of victory. What a rush that was; man, that was indescribable. The rush was unbelievable; I can see where thrill searchers get off on this stuff. It can be a real trip.

We drifted on downriver, navigating small sections of white water and really having a great ride. We paddled a section called the Blackwell still water, which is well named—not much ride, just paddle. At the Blackwell dam, we made camp, and what a horror that was: black flies and millions and billions of them. There was only one thing to do: go to bed and cover your head. After dark, we'll build a fire and get a bite to eat. After dark, the flies were gone, and it was tolerable to sit by the fire to talk and laugh about our trip so far. We had two more days to complete the trip, and we were all excited and ready for the challenge.

"What the hell was that?" My kayak exploded just sitting there, no one even near it. *What am I going to do now?* No repair kit, no pump, no nothing. *Man, this white water stuff can be a pain in my ass.*

The morning brought a new plan. Again, I jumped in with Eric and negotiated the river down to the goolie club, where we disembarked the river and our second shot. But we're not done yet. We'll hit her again July 4, another long weekend—three days to try it again.

On July 4th weekend, I'll give you one guess where I was. Back in Newcome, looking at the Hudson River again. This time with two inner tubes sandwiched between two pieces of plywood, oarlocks to row and keep her straight come white water. The weather was just beautiful, the fishing never better, but the river too low again. We had four boats; again, one boat was destroyed before the goolie club, another one gone shortly after, and the walk out for their captains, myself and Bob, continued on down through a beautiful section of river known as the Blue Ledges. Once you're in, there's only one way out down stream. The end of the day found us at the beginning of the Harris Rift and again one more boat limping to shore. The Blue Ledges took her toll and left us with one choice, hike out over the mountain to the road and to a truck in the north creek.

My boat was still in good shape, so I took it into the woods and buried it and buried the paddles in another spot to wait for my return in the fall when the water would be higher and navigation of the Harris Rift would be possible.

I made plans to return in September and return I did with my good friend Bob Ackley—a friend, I might add, who has never run white water. My plan was to go in on the railroad tracks to the trestle and make camp there Friday night, hike upriver above the Harris Rift Saturday, ride my boat back to camp, spend the night, and complete the ride Sunday. Friday night found us making camp at the railroad trestle. We had a great meal of canned ham and potatoes, more than we could eat. A small piece of ham remained in the can by the fire as we drank our coffee and visited as anyone would do. All of a sudden, a limb crack and a movement to my left. Bob looked up; it's a coon, just lying still and watching him. This guy had no fear of us at all. He walked right between us and the fire, picked up that last small piece of ham, and left—just as if we had invited him.

The next morning, I was awakened by a much larger noise, and all I could think of was, *Bear!* I dug my way out of my sleeping bag on a dead run and headed for the river. Bob jumped up with a, "What's wrong?" "There's a bear out here!" I yelled. And he was right behind me. Neither one of us saw a bear, but I didn't take any chances.

After breakfast, we headed upstream above the Harris Rift, where I had left my boat in July, but it was gone. Bob asked if I was sure this was the spot; after all, it's a big woods. "I'm sure. I'll prove it." I buried my paddles in another spot, and they were there just the way I left them.

I came prepared this time, thinking a porcupine might chew my tubes, so I brought new ones. We inflated them and tied a two by twelve board we found at this campsite to the two tubes and were ready to ride the Harris Rift back to camp. As I mentioned before, Bob had no white water savvy and was a little apprehensive, I might add. Not only that, but it had rained every day the week before we came, and the Hudson River was rolling at twelve feet, seven inches, and I mean rolling.

We mapped some of our route downstream while we walked up to find my boat. Being very concerned, Bob wanted to stay close to shore until he got his feet wet, if you know what I mean. So stay close we did until we made the corner and looked the rift in the eye. I said, "This is where we must get to the other side, remember?" So we headed for the opposite shore and with little effort on my part, according to Bob. "We're not going to make it," I yelled. "Straighten her up, we're going in!" And in we went. At times, our makeshift boat went under so far only my head remained out of the water, diving again and again and again. All you could see was white. We were swallowed up by river and paddling just to keep her straight. Our intense ride lasted maybe four minutes, four minutes of pure rage. We escaped the rift in one piece and not sure of our route through the next section of the river. Bob wanted to survey it before making our run, so we headed for shore. Big mistake. We headed for shore, but the current was so strong it took us downstream into a tree leaning over the river. The limbs were so low I had to lie back to get under them. When Bob laid back, he went off the back into the river and dumped us. I never let go of my paddle. I was under for only a second. When I surfaced, the raft was right in front of me. I threw my arm over the edge of the tube and turned to look for Bob. A moment later, his feet came up right beside me, and I quickly reached deep into the raging river and grabbed him by the collar and pulled him up. Gasping for air and spitting water, Bob said, "A man could get killed out here." As one could, that's a fact. Bob spotted his paddle, grabbed it, and we finished our drive to shore. We surveyed the next section of river and made the remaining ride to camp without any trouble. Camp greeted us with warm dry clothes and a good stiff drink of rye and water. The next day, Bob wanted to carry out instead of ride, simply to make the drive home in dry clothes instead of wet ones. So that's what we did.

At other times, I have hiked in to the Blue Ledges and the Harris Rift, usually the last weekend in September for a relaxing weekend in the woods. The Hudson River is a beautiful but yet very demanding and dangerous place. If you like, check it out but be ready for the worst.

Chapter 14

THE FARM

It's 7:00 AM, December 15. Jenny and I just boarded a flight headed for Hawaii to visit my daughter and her family there for Christmas. As we were walking through the airport, an old friend asked if I got my buck. With a question like that, I am always sent right back into hunting season. A smile will instantly come across my face. Like most men of the woods, I love to talk and listen of tales of the seasons past.

I am reminded of the many seasons Jenny and I have spent on Jim's farm in the southern tier. Jim is my cousin. We spent many a summer growing up at his house, my house, you know how it works. As the years have passed, hunting season has kept us in touch. The time of year that says, "Drop everything and get your butt down here. There's deer to hunt." And it's OK, and I'm on my way!

Wandering on the farm, I found what I considered to be a good watch on the top of the hill, the highest point of the farm—a giant tree sitting in the corner of a hedgerow with a cornfield to my west and south and pasture to my northeast. The tree was so big it was hard to climb, but once up about fifteen feet, I found a very comfortable place to sit. Here in this tree are some great memories.

A quiet morning, opening the day, I nestled in my tree; I'm listening to the sounds of shotguns going off all around me. With my field glasses, I can see for almost a half mile in any direction. I'm perched with my pistol and my late father's single-shot twenty gauge. It's been an average morning. I have viewed deer on two hillsides but too far for me to even think about but always nice to see, keeps you on your toes, if you know what I mean. As I'm glassing the edges of the cornfield, excitement hits, bang. *What's this, a buck! About 120 yards out!* His nose in the air, checking for the scent of anything strange or the presence of danger. He must be feeling safe;

he begins to move from west to east. A closer look at his rack tells me he's a very wide-racked crotch horn, probably fourteen to sixteen-inch spread and eighteen months old. As he gets midfield, I feel he's as close as he's going to get, about eighty yards; and that's just about the limit of this gun, just an old single shot with a single bead for a sight. I'm leaning against the tree, holding her as steady as I can. Luck is in my corner the buck stops and looks away. I'm rocked slightly as the slug's velocity is released from the gun. Almost instantly, the buck leaps into the air. Frantically, he runs a small 360 degrees and into the standing corn. With an enthusiastic gesture of my right arm, I whispered, "Yes." I'm confident of my shot. With my field glasses in hand, I looked for any action in the field. Five minutes, ten minutes, nothing. Carefully down out of the tree, I headed for the spot I last saw the buck, a spot well marked and easy to find. The buck barely entered the corn before giving it all up, a well-placed shot with almost instant effect. Now with field dressing complete, a decision has to be made: drag him to the road then walk to the farm or just drag him. With David just down the hill, I opted to drag—not far, maybe five hundred yards. I made the drag to within a hundred yards of his stand when I noticed no David. *Well, Bill is just through the hedge; he'll help me.* I dragged for another two hundred yards and, guess what, no Bill. Well, if I go across this field to the next hedge, I will find Rich, Jim, and Jenny in the next field. So I continued my drag, and by now all I have on is my shirt, I started sweating way back at David's stand. I managed the drag all the way across that field and dropped the buck in near exhaustion. I stepped through the hedge with field glasses in hand. I looked for Rich, no Rich. Then for Jim, no Jim. And then way in the far corner of the field was Jenny. Praise the Lord, I can always count on Jenny. Looking through my field glasses, I whistled as loud as I can whistle. *Bingo.* She heard me. I gave her an arm motion for her to come, then watched her again. *Message received.* Jenny climbed out of her stand and headed my way. Twenty minutes later, she arrived, excited to assist me in the final leg of my drag. Well, as I said, I can always count on Jenny.

Another year perched in my famous tree, I was determined to harvest a deer with my pistol. To be sure of this, I carried no long gun at all, just my .44 Magnum with a four-power scope. After spending many hours at my range, I'm sure I can make a clean shot. On this particular morning, action begins early. A doe steps from the corn not forty yards away. Confident, I pulled the .44 from its nest under my arm, cocked the hammer, rested my arms over a limb, and placed the crosshairs on the mark. My ears began ringing after the bark of my .44. The results are instant and the deer is mine. After last year, I decided to drag my game the short distance to the road, hide her there, and walk to the farm. After retrieving my deer, Jim came up to the house to get the truck. He said, "Jenny got one, so get in." I jumped into the truck, and across the field we went. Bouncing across the field as if we were taking a swamp tour with an occasional, "I-EE," along with an outburst of laughter, we managed to actually make it to our destination. Oh, to remember the good times. Jenny harvested a fine doe bigger than the one we just put in the tree. Jim laughs as he tells me she was sleeping. "I had to yell, 'Jen,' to wake her up." Jenny says, "I wasn't sleeping, just daydreaming a little." She told us that there were three of them, a buck and two does, all on the run. Jenny made a fine shot, took the heart out of a running deer. She was going to try again for the buck, but they were too far away. Besides, they were headed right for David. Guess what, no David. We dressed out the deer, loaded it into the truck, and bounced our way back to the farm.

After lunch and a few laughs, I made my way back up the hill to my tree. After being perched for a couple of hours, a neighbor came by and told me he had just seen a buck so keep my eyes open. The neighbor had only been gone about ten minutes when I noticed the buck northeast to my rear. I quickly pulled my pistol. My heart began to race. From this position, I had nothing to use for a bench rest. I was forced to make my shot completely off hand. The buck had his nose to the ground and probably had doe on his mind. This was my first season completely relying on my pistol, which was stimulating my heart to beat even faster, and it seemed even louder. A quick guess gave the buck about a seventy-five-yard gap between us. I cocked the hammer, lowered the crosshairs, and touched it off. Nothing, no response at all from the buck. I cocked it again. The loud roar had no effect on the buck at all. He continued walking with his nose to the ground. I fired again. This time, he gave a quick kick as I assumed the bullet passed very close. Still, he continued walking, nose to the ground. I made one more quick shot as my heart is now pounding so hard it's barely staying in my chest. I cocked the hammer for the fifth time and remember I never reloaded after taking a doe this morning. This is it—slow down, squeeze the trigger, and don't pull it. This is my last chance. The crosshairs are firm on his shoulder—take a breath, hold it, and squeeze. My .44 roared once again. Instantly, the buck folded and laid motionless, better than eighty yards away. My ears are ringing from the percussion of five rounds, one after another. I descended my perch and made my way to the buck. While admiring my take, David and Gary came around a corner in the hedge and congratulated me. When I pointed out my watch, they were amazed at the distance for a pistol shot. I commented it would have been better if I could have calmed down first. I call it the heat of the moment when the adrenaline is pumping, and all you can think of is, *Shoot, or he will get away.* Again, I made the drag to the road with David's help and walked to the farm for a truck. This made three in the tree for Jenny and I, a fine eight-point buck and two does. Not a bad day on the farm, not bad at all.

The next weekend, Jenny and I found ourselves back on the farm. Jenny still had her buck tag and wanted to try my tree. It was a cold morning, and snow was on the ground. My tree, as I mentioned in the beginning, was on the very top of the hill with no break from the wind. We completed the trek up the hill, and I assisted Jenny up the tree. I ask her if she was all set, and I went back to the farm. Before I got my coffee poured, Jenny came through the door, frozen. "It's cold up there," she said. "Yes, it sure is and nowhere to get out of the wind either," I said. So the rest of that season was spent in front of the fireplace with a bowl of chili and a cup of coffee.

I've always been thankful for hunting season. It's that one time of year when we say, "No, I'm not working today. I'm going hunting down on the farm with my family and friends."

Chapter 15

CANOEING

I have come to the realization that if you want to see a man and woman, boy and girl, or husband and wife get into a fight, all you have to do is put them in the same canoe together. I cannot possibly tell you how many miles have passed under my canoe, but the number is high. Some of my greatest outdoor memories are connected to a canoe. Just the sheer tranquility is enough to make you never want to go home.

My daughter, Steph, spent many summer weekends in the middle of our seventeen-foot aluminum along with my two chocolate Labs and gear enough for the weekend—whether it be two, three, or four days. On one such weekend, Jenny and I decided to explore the Oswegatchie from inlet to high falls, a winding up stream paddle, but mostly a deepwater trip. We managed to get into the water late morning, along with a few other canoes and kayakers. We paddled along with them for a couple of hours, then seemed to just leave them behind. We made camp at a lean-to about halfway to the falls. Steph, of course, needed a swim while Jenny and I made camp. I checked the map and realized we were about halfway to the falls. I figured we could be there by noon with an early start; then it would be downstream all the way to the truck. She agreed, and we would attempt it, weather permitting. Morning dawned—a beautiful day, so upstream to the falls we went. We encountered small ripples in the stream, nothing we couldn't navigate without getting out—just get on your knees and pull all the water you can. Noon found us having lunch at the falls—boiled hot dogs, my favorite. We enjoyed sitting on shore dangling our feet in the water and watching the falls; it was beautiful, to say the least. But our quiet lunch was quickly disrupted when Jenny screamed and yanked her foot from the water. "What the hell!" I yelled. "My toe, my toe!" she screamed.

I quickly looked, and a crab was dangling off her little toe. I pulled him off as quick as I could and dropped him in the boiling water. "Can you catch a few more?" I asked. "Just one isn't enough." "No! Jerk! You want more? Catch them on *your* toe!"

The paddle back was long, as you might guess. Eighteen miles back, to be exact. By evening, our shoulders were sore as were our backs. I looked around every corner, hoping to see our truck, and, when we finally found it, we had paddled twenty-six miles that day; about eight miles were upstream. A task I don't soon want to repeat.

When Steph would ask if she could take along a friend, it was never a problem. We would take another canoe—one for Jenny and one for me—and the girls would help paddle. We decided to explore Racket Lake. My friend, Bill Fergison, and his wife, Lee, joined us, but they brought their seven-and-one-half-horse boat. Bill found a beach to camp at and radioed back to me where to go. It was an easy paddle. The wind was at our backs, and it took us almost all the way to the Forked Lake portage. I decided we had missed the spot. I asked a cottage owner where the beach was, and he instructed me to go back against the wind and around the point. It was the only beach on the lake. As the waves continued to grow, Jenny became unable to move forward against them. She became convinced she would surely dump it if she continued. Concerned for their safety, I had her stay on the shore while Steph and I looked for Bill. It was not the easiest, but we managed a forward movement against twelve-to-fourteen-inch waves. We found Bill and Lee and returned to Jenny and Jess, then towed their canoe to the beach where we made camp. I think she called me a jerk.

A trip seven miles upstream from Axton Landing to Racket Falls was Stephanie and Jessica's first attempt to do it alone. We left Axton, and Jenny and I paddled for thirty minutes and pulled over to shore, then waited for the girls while we drank a soda. Thirty minutes later, we decided we should go looking for them; and twenty minutes after that, we found them. They were checking out both sides of the river, and, of course, it was the other one's fault. So Jenny took Jess, and I took Steph, or they would still be out there blaming each other and going nowhere.

Steph, my dog Mandy, and I completed the seven-mile paddle, unloaded our gear, made camp, and then returned to the river's edge to wait for Jenny, Jess, and our other Lab, Sadie, and enjoyed a cold soda while we waited. Another camper in a motorboat came alongside and said, "A lady with a dog just like that said to wait up." "OK," I said. "Thanks, I'll wait right here." And so I did. She called me jerk again.

We were caught by surprise on a three-day trip in '87 at Paul Smith's College. Our plan for the weekend was to paddle to the base of St. Regis Mountain on Saturday, make camp, and climb the mountain on Sunday and make the return paddle on Monday, the Fourth of July. A beautiful Saturday morning, sunshine and warm air; it's a great day for a paddle. A party of five canoes was expected, but one party was extremely late, so Keith remained behind to show them the way. Stephanie took his spot with Jaime, and we shoved off. The paddle would be about two hours if all went well, starting in Lower Saint Regis Lake through Spitfire, then into Upper Saint Regis Lake, then past the Emily Post Estate into a narrow flow to the base of the mountain, where two Adirondack lean-tos awaited our arrival. As we began our trip across the first lake, Jenny said she needed to make a nature call, so we pointed our vessel toward Rabbit Island, and the air was suddenly filled with screams. Twisting on my seat to look behind me, I saw the bottom of the red canoe as it was turning over. "OH SHIT!" Karen and Pat were in the water. We turned our canoe 180 degrees and raced back to help. A fifteen-foot rubber canoe I use for white water with plenty of flotation had no danger of sinking, so just hold on to it, and you'll be fine. When Jenny and I arrived, it was ugly—gear floating around and bodies in the water, Karen just holding the canoe, and Pat, a smoker, held the canoe with one hand and her cigarettes over her head with the other. If they go down, I'm sure she's going down after them. Bill and Jaime were retrieving gear while Jenny and I pondered our best solution to the problem. Shore is only eighty yards away, so swim your canoe to shallow water; then, refloat it while the rest of your gear is pulled from its watery grave. Karen lost her boom box and some tapes, and Pat lost her fishing pole. They managed to find a dry change of cloths, reloaded their boat, and climbed in to give it another try. The remainder of the trip was uneventful in comparison to the circus we just witnessed. There were many beautiful summer homes in the area and landscapes to match.

At camp, tents were soon pitched and firewood gathered, more than normal, because there was a dryer we had to run to dry a few damp articles like clothes and sleeping bags that took a swim.

Day 2 found us at the top of Saint Regis Mountain, taking in the view of a spectacular scene; lakes and waterways lay at our feet in between smaller rolling hills and, in the distance, the high peaks of the Adirondacks, breathtaking at the very least. At this time, the fire tower is still standing, but I'm unsure of its fate; so many of the towers have been removed to step aside as progress moves forward, and satellites keep a watchful eye on our forest lands. While at the top, we enjoyed our lunch as we took a break and enjoyed the view over God's tapestry.

There are always some great moments around camp. Here, we enjoyed a great game of hide-and-seek, and then, with no warning, we were entertained by a terrific fireworks display form the Post Estate. They must have known we were coming. Usually, the dark sky gives us a clear view of the stars, and the bonfire is always the scene of good conversation.

On our return voyage, Pat took the bow with me, and Karen joined Jenifer in her canoe, hopefully to avoid another dunking. There is nothing worse than a wet ride home. We were all packed up when Keith took a pack and headed into the woods. Pat asked where he was going. "To put that pack in the truck," replied Jaime, and Pat hit the ceiling. "I paddled all the way here, almost drowned, and you tell me there is a road over there? I think I need my head examined."

Jenny and I managed to convince a couple of friends to join us for a long weekend of canoeing on the same trip from Axton Landing to Racket Falls. Kevin and Diane are workaholics; if they're not on the job, they're working on their farm. Work, work, work. As far as I'm concerned, there's more to life. To get them into a canoe, we first took them on a day trip downstream from South Landing Bridge to Lake View Beach for a picnic lunch. Jenny took Kevin, and I took Diane. All went well until Kevin tried to splash me and broke his paddle, snapped it right in two. It was a good reason why I always carry a spare. Later in the day, a big carp came up and hit my canoe right beside Diane. I swear she went two feet straight up. She managed to show some restraint, which was a good thing because I was sure she was going to walk on water. Up on the Racket again, Kevin rode bow for Jenny, and Diane was in front of my boat. About noon, we decided to stop for lunch, Kevin pulled the bow of their canoe up, and Jenny stepped out. The river was waist deep. Jenny had one foot in and one foot out. It amazed me the canoe didn't tip over, or Jenny got wetter than she did. After lunch, Kevin and Diane wanted to try it together. "OK," I said, "Good luck." It wasn't long before it started. "You're supposed to steer back there." "Shut up, hag bag." "Bite me." "Shut up to me." "Terry, help him; he's so stupid." "You're doing it." Need I say more about getting into a fight? My response was, "You'll figure it out or kill each other trying."

We managed to get to camp about 3:30-4:00, and Kevin and Diane were both still breathing. We pitched our tents and made our surroundings to fit our style when I noticed Kevin and Diane had pillows. "Pillows," I said. "You don't bring pillows when you go camping; you roll your pants up and stick them under your head." And when Kevin wasn't looking, I stole them and put them in my tent. It wasn't long before he noticed. "Where are my pillows?" He yelled and headed straight for my tent. "What the hell is this, Diane?" shouted Kevin. "They have a queen-size air mattress in here, and he's bitching about my pillows and had nerve enough to steal them."

Day 2 was a short trip up to the falls—where I took some pictures, had lunch, and enjoyed the falls. Kevin and Diane seemed to really enjoy themselves and found out what it's like to relax.

Day 3 found us breaking camp and heading downstream. As the trip progressed, they got better but still swore at each other all the way to the truck.

Another trip with Kevin and Diane on the Racket found me answering questions from Diane on what to do if your canoe tips over. How do you refloat it or get back in? So I told her I would show her some tricks when we made camp. We found a nice spot with a real deep hole right in front. I told Diane to put on her life jacket, and I would show her a few things. I also had Jenny bring the other canoe. In the middle of the river, I quickly dumped the canoe and instantly lit her fire. The words from her mouth weren't meant for my virgin ears. "You son of a bitch, I wasn't ready. I'll kick your ass." She called me everything in the book but jerk. She denies it but even took a swing at me. I, on the other hand, was laughing so hard she couldn't hurt me if she caught me. Jenny came alongside Diane, and I slid our canoe up onto Jenny's, bottom side up. With all the water out, we turned it over and back into the river. "Now, you on one side and me on the other; we get in at the same time. Ready, go," I quickly was up and over the edge of the canoe, but Diane couldn't do it. All she could do was laugh. At one point, she had one leg and one arm in my canoe and one leg and one arm in Jenny's canoe. We were all laughing so hard it's a wonder we didn't capsize them again. Good times had by all.

As we all know, time flies, and the years just slip away. Now we have three grandchildren that have joined in on all the fun if Mom and Dad survive the paddle.

Labor Day 2001 was their first outing, canoeing, or camping for grandchildren, Travis and Jessica. Together with Mom and Dad, Rachel, my second daughter, and her husband, Travis, they joined us for a three-day weekend on Long Lake. We paddled in about three miles to Kelly Point and made camp there. Along for the ride in our canoe were our Labs, Sadie and Mandy. We took up residence in a lean-to while Rachel and Travis pitched a tent. The rest of the day was spent swimming and a game of hide-and-seek, which is always fun, and the kids feel right at home. Later, the gang came over to the lean-to for a bonfire and somemores; I got a ration of shit from Travis over my air mattress. It seems I was complaining about their pillows. What is it about pillows, anyway? Rachel had a good time even though a mouse ran between her legs at the bonfire, and another was running around under her tent in the middle of the night.

A hike up Kempshall Mountain was the plan for the second day, but the trail has grown over and hasn't been maintained since they removed the fire tower. We got close but no cigar. It was a good walk anyway.

Did I mention that Travis is in the navy? Well, he is, and they now live in Florida. They came home in June this year, '03, for a three-week vacation and wanted to go canoe camping again, so I planned a three-day trip for the Fourth of July weekend. On this trip, grandson Owen joined us for his very first trip. Kevin and Diane and their two grandchildren also joined us, and we put in at Wannakena and then canoed down the Oswegatchie to Cranberry Lake and up Dead Creek Flow. Here, we found a campsite and set up housekeeping for the next three days. The paddle was a short three and a half to four miles, all deepwater. Kevin and Diane are getting better; but occasionally you'll hear Diane say, "Are you paddling back there?" "And Kevin would reply, "NO, you told me to steer, so that's what I'm doing." Then they started laughing at Rachel and Travis. "We thought we were bad, but they're going to kill each other on the way or when they hit shore, one or the other." See what I mean? The best of friends until you put them in a canoe together. And if I'm not mistaken, Rachel even called him a jerk. It's funny how things get passed on.

Camp was a great spot. The kids had a place to swim, room to run, play, and explore; and the expression on their faces when they all caught fish was priceless.

I had planned a hike up Cat Mountain for the middle day, and, when we headed out, the kids just took off; it was hard to slow them down. Their excitement and anticipation was heartwarming for me to see. I can only hope they take an interest in the great outdoors. I estimated we got about a third of the way up the mountain when three of the four kids we had with us all complained they were tired and needed to be carried. So up on our shoulders they went and rode all the way back to camp, where they miraculously regained their energy.

Of course, big Travis had to challenge me to a race. He ran from our campsite, around the point to Jannix Landing while I paddled straight across. He's in real good shape but just not good enough. You know what they say, "Close, but no cigar."

Labor Day '03, grandson Owen joined us again for another three-day trip along with Kevin and Diane and also with Jenny's sister, Jaime, and her husband, Keith. Keith has joined me on a few hunts in the past, you may remember.

We explored the Cold River up as far as we could paddle and made camp at Calkins Creek lean-to. The night was clear and a bit cool. There was not a cloud in the sky and the stars were shining bright. No streetlights out here. On this trip, we must portage around Racket Falls, so pack light. Everything you have, you'll have to carry. Our dinning entrees consisted of freeze-dried food. We all had different kinds, and different meals so it was. "I'll taste yours, and you taste mine." Owen was once again happy to catch fish. He would lit right up and reel him in. "I got one, Grampa, see." And he would jump up and down.

Day 2 was a real easy ride downstream—peaceful and quiet, taking pictures of ducks and landscape. Then we hit the falls. I got my canoe ready, bungeed in my life jackets, and taped in my paddles while Jaime and Jenny put Owen's pack on him; then Keith and Jaime headed up the trail. I helped Jenny finish up her pack and sent her and Owen, who, I might add, is only four on their way up the trail. Diane was ready to go, so I gave Kevin a hand getting his canoe on his shoulders, and away they went. After putting on my day pack, I donned my canoe and headed up the trail for a short-mile walk around Racket Falls. Keith and Jaime made it to the other end first. They're still young and always seem to have their shit together, if you know what I mean. I managed to make it to the other end ahead of Jenny and Owen. After putting my canoe down, I, along with Jaime, headed back to give some assistance to the others. Keith stayed with our gear. As we headed up the trail, Jenny and Owen were headed down, and he had the biggest smile on his face you could ever imagine. "I did it, Grampa, I did it." "Yes, you did. I'm so proud of you." Oh man, that really made my day. With a lot of encouragement from Gramma, Owen had managed to walk all the way, carrying his own pack. Jaime and I found Kevin and Diane up on the trail, tuffing it out, and gave a little assistance. After all, this was their first portage, and it's not an easy one. All did well. Day 3 found us getting off the river at Axton Landing and saying good-bye to Keith and Jaime as they headed back to Massachusetts. The summer is over. Our schedules don't allow us another trip before fall and winter will set in. All we can do is start planning for next year. Jenny and I have four canoes. Each has different purposes. The seventeen-foot aluminum we call the Barge will easily hold two adults, two kids, and two dogs with all your gear. The sixteen-foot fiberglass, we call our portage canoe. We take it when we go light and portage. The fifteen-foot rubber canoe is the one we run white water with. If we hit rock, there is never any damage done. The twelve-foot fiberglass I like to take when I go alone or with my dog. It's just the right size.

I have in my plans to complete the 266-mile trip from Old Forge, New York, to Paul Smith's College one way and a route change for the trip back. A trip that I plan to follow in the footsteps of the writer George Sears took in the 1800s. I also have plans to paddle the 750 miles from Port Kent, Maine, to Old Forge, New York, a trip just completed this year, 2003, in fifty-six days by a solo canoeist. I'm sure I will find plenty to write about and take pictures of on these two trips. So if you're looking to go canoeing in either of these two areas, maybe, just maybe, we'll bump into each other, have some coffee, and tell a tale or two. Till then, keep your canoe straight and a smile on your face because out here there are plenty to smile about.

Chapter 16

BACKPACKING

It's a whole different prospective when you carry everything you need on your back. Whether you are just going on a day hike and just carry your lunch and water or plan a six-month trip on the Appalachian Trail, you carry what you need. Most of the time, you will start out with too much gear and quickly realize, *I don't need that damn thing,* and discard it at your earliest opportunity. Such was the case in a book I read about two men walking the trail from Georgia to Maine. Most of their gear was lost in the first seven miles. I guess they didn't need any frills: they even tossed their coffee filters and then filtered their coffee through toilet paper. If I had a choice, I guess they made the right one.

On a weekend trip a few years back, daughters Rachel and Steph found Jen and I on about a four-mile hike into Round Pond from Aldrich—mostly a level hike, no real mountains to climb or rivers to cross, just carry what you need from point A to point B and enjoy the landscape in-between. There's a whole different world out there, and backpacking is a great way to see it. Everyone made the hike and discovered a beautiful small private lake, and the only access was to walk in. We made camp and gathered firewood for the evening bonfire, then hit the lake for a refreshing swim.

Around the bonfire, cooking hot dogs for supper gave us a chance to catch up on what's going on in Rachel's world. We don't see much of her since Rachel's mother and I split. Technically, she is my stepdaughter. We laughed, sang songs, and even went for a moonlight swim, then hit the hay. Sleep was interrupted by a thunderstorm; and, man, did it rain buckets? Cats and dogs too. Soon there was a chatter coming from the kids' tent. "Are you getting wet?" I said. "Yes." "Do you want to come over here?" "Yes." "Well, you can't." "DAD!" "OK, come on." And they crawled in with us.

Morning brought sunshine and a breeze to dry out with—pack up and head out, making memories of another great weekend.

Another hike to Round Pond, we headed in from the Harrisville side in Jenny's blazer, taking a four-wheel drive trail as far as we could. Steve, Ann, Jenny, and I came to a spot called Jenny's Creek. It was probably eighty yards across and water backed up by a beaver dam. Steve and I decided to check it out before driving across. I started ripping holes in the dam, and Steve walked across the dam and back with news that it was only sixteen inches deep, so we can just drive across. We went back to the blazer and started driving across. Soon, the blazer started pushing a wall of water, and the girls were laughing and making claims on the sunroof, which one would crawl out first. Laughter changed to screams when the blazer dropped in, and water went over the hood and up the windshield. With an, "Oh shit!" I gave it the gas; and the blazer came up, and we made it across. I was sure we were done. Jenny said, "Don't get stuck. I have no signal on my cell phone." After the creek, the road quickly began closing in. We soon had to park it and continue on foot. It was early spring, and we discovered wildflowers of many kinds and a whole covey of partridge chicks. Mom, the hen, gave us the old broken-wing trick, and all disappeared. The walk was about four miles to the pond, and, again, it was all ours. Walking in the warm spring air was fine, but when we stopped, we were invaded by blackflies, real nasty bugs that leave a three-day itch when they bite. Steve packed MREs (meals ready to eat) for lunch. Ann didn't think she would care for them so don't pack any for her. But when Steve started the stove to boil the water, Ann was the first in line. I think she walked up an appetite. She even said they were good. All too soon, it was time to go. We must once again leave this wonderful, quiet, secluded spot and return to the real world. Back at the blazer after we walked eight miles, the creek had subsided quite a lot, and driving back across was no problem.

On a three-day trip in the days before Jenny, I took another "friend," if you know what I mean, hiking to the Harris Rift on the Hudson River, an annual trip I made on the last weekend of September for many years. We made camp and enjoyed short-day hikes and returned to camp and talked around the campfire as we cooked our evening entree of whatever was light and easy to carry. In the middle of the night, she complained of being cold. We were in a double sleeping bag, so I lit a candle lantern, pulled up my knees, and placed the lantern by my legs. In a while, when we warmed up, I took the lantern out and we were warm the rest of the night. The next night was a repeat of the night before. She complained of being cold, so I repeated the candle lantern trick, lit the lantern, and placed it beside my knees. Soon I had the feeling it was "hot" in here. I had fallen asleep, the candle had burned down and out of the lantern, and my sleeping bag was now on fire. With an, "OH SHIT!" I began slapping the fire to put it out. Now I have a hole in my bag. "Dumb, right? Right." But neither of us got burnt, and it tickled our funny bone.

I made another mistake in the same geological area but on a different September and also with a different "friend." We hiked beside the railroad tracks to the trestle then followed the river upstream to where I like to make camp. We made camp, and it began to rain and rain. It rained for three days, and everything was wet, even the toilet paper; so as far as I'm concerned we have a problem. I decided to pack up and head over the top of the mountain instead of walking around the way we came in. Good plan, right? Nope, bad plan, because I didn't bring a compass, and with it raining, there's no sun. As we followed the trail up the mountain, it poured. Lightning, thunder—you name it; it was hitting us from every angle. There's no point in making camp; everything is soaked so just keep going. We made it to the top of the mountain, a spot that can be very confusing. I told my "friend" to stay there, and I would find the ribbon that marks the trail on the other side then call her. I looked for a while and found a ribbon and called her over. The trail was completely hidden. I showed her the ribbon and opened the brush, and there was the trail. With no relief in the weather, we kept going down and down the mountain, and to my surprise, it was the same side we walked up, all the way back to the river. Well, no point in stopping here. We might as well go out the way we came in. So don't put your pack down yet; it's going to be dark before we get our butts back to the truck because of my screwup. On our way out, the brooks we crossed coming in were now raging rivers. We had to go upstream until we could find a place to cross. Most of the time, a downed tree was our bridge to the other side. I couldn't remember ever being this wet, my shoes were just like a sponge, and there was not a dry spot on my wrinkled, pruned-up body. So remember: if you don't need a compass, take two.

On a recent trip to Arizona to visit Steve and Ann, the four of us took a short-day hike to Massacre Mesa, a spot where the Apache Indians attacked and killed some of the Mexicans mining in the Superstition Mountains. This forced the Mexicans to hide their gold and run back to Mexico. It was later believed the old Dutchman found this stash and so became the tales of the lost Dutchman gold mine. It was said he would leave Phoenix, go to his mine, and return with gold but was never gone long enough to actually do any mining. So tales that he had found the Mexican gold were spread, and to this day others still search.

The next day, Steve and I took a seven-mile hike to Garden Valley to some Indian ruins. Here, we found some small pieces of broken pottery. Then on to an old gold mine, we found off the trail. I entered the mine and walked in as far as I dared with no light. It was quite dark but real interesting. We wondered, *What kind of determination does it take to work this hard, and why did he dig here? What was so special about this spot?* After taking some pictures, we headed back to the trail. We then discovered Hackleberry Spring. A hole hammered out in the side of a solid rock wall, there was a pipe hanging out, and the water was running. The book we had told us that this spring runs all-year long, and, believe me, it was cold and good. Walking back to the truck completed our seven-mile loop and brought back memories of when Steve and Ann lived in New York, and we took many day hikes in the Adirondack Mountains—such as Jenny's Creek, Bear Mountain, Cat Mountain, and many more—trips we took to enjoy and discover nature.

On a recent trip to Massachusetts, Keith and Jamie took Jenny and I up part of the Appalachian Trail to the top of Mount Evert, the vista at the top was breathtaking. This has inspired me to walk part of the trail, so plans are being made for me, and I hope Steve, to walk the trail for about thirty days. I'm sure it will be an experience I won't soon forget. How about you, wanna go for a walk?

Chapter 17

ARIZONA ELK

I'm in the airport, waiting for my flight to Pittsburgh, the first leg of my trip to Arizona. My plan is to hunt elk with my bow and arrow on the Mullion Rim. As of now, I'm a day late. My flights have been canceled for one reason or another. Today is September 15, Tuesday. The twin towers in New York City collapsed after a terrorist attack, so things have been on edge ever since. We talked about shipping my equipment ahead to avoid being lost by the airline but decided there shouldn't be a problem. After getting my boarding passes, they had to inspect all of my gear, and I mean all! My only consolation, I felt, was the fact that I am bow hunting and didn't have any firearms. Every airline person I had to talk to asked the same question, "Is that a rifle?" Of course, my answer was, "No, it's a bow and arrow." To my amazement, the only thing they wanted to confiscate were my peanuts. Considering the circumstances, everyone was very friendly and apologized for any inconvenience. I responded, "No problem," on my part. They have a job to do, and I would like to get there in one piece.

The plans for this trip began a year and a half ago when Jenny and I vacationed in Arizona with Steve and Ann. Steve has hunted with me prior, on four hunts you may remember: two bear hunts, an elk hunt, and a caribou hunt. Plus he has joined me in the swamp for whitetail. While visiting, Steve invited me to join him for elk in Arizona. "You won't have to ask me twice." I said; and the seed was planted, and plans began to grow. Unable to make it that year, we hoped it would all come together the next.

Arizona only gives nonresidents less than 10 percent of its tags. Steve suggested we apply for cow tags. It would be our best chance, being nonresidents and without a guide. So, of course, that's what we did, and then the waiting game began. While I waited, I took my bow off the wall and a close inspection indicated I needed a new string. My good friend Bill offered to fix it for me, and he did. Bill also has joined me on many hunts: bear, caribou, whitetail in the swamp, on the farm, and in the Adirondacks. In fact, Bill had his eye on a nice twelve-point buck in the swamp but was unable to get a clear shot and refused to try and possibly wound and waste that magnificent animal.

Bill returned my bow to me, and I began shooting. I was shocked at my ability to draw my bow. My god, I was only able to shoot sixteen arrows a day, and the last four were work, and I mean work. I threw my back out of place twice, I began to get some swelling in my left elbow, and my neck became tight. I decided I just can't do this anymore. I was in my hot tub every night, massaging my back, and then going to bed. I called Randy. You remember him? Randy, John, and I shot five challenge cup tournaments in one year and won four of them. I asked him if he could turn my bow down; it's causing me problems, and I must be ready to hunt in just two months whether it be for elk or just whitetails. Randy laughed just like he always does and said, "Sure, bring it over. We'll turn it down and paper test it too."

When I arrived, Randy asked me, "How many pounds are you pulling?" "Seventy-two," I responded. "And how much do you want to turn it down?" "Well, the way I feel right now, sixty-two would be good." Randy put my bow on the scales, and to my amazement, it rolled over at eighty-one pounds. "Holy shit, Ter. Nobody pulls eighty pounds!" And he began to laugh again. "Well, I can't pull it either." Randy turned it down to seventy-four pounds and said, "Try that, Ter." "Well, that's a piece of cake," I said. Must be when Bill changed the string, he set it to eighty-one pounds instead of seventy-one pounds. "Man, do I feel better? I thought I became a wimp over the winter."

I just boarded my flight to Pittsburgh. Maybe I'll get there yet. Oh yeah, we're airborne.

Where was I? Oh yeah, the next day I returned to my practice range, and to my amazement, shooting was once again a dream. No effort at all, and my groups were softball size at fifty yards. After a couple of weeks of that, it was time to affix a broadhead and resight my bow. Because I'm hunting elk, I must use a fixed blade with a one-inch back, which means I must take off the seventy-five-grain collapsible I was using for whitetail. My choice for this hunt is eighty-five-grain thunderheads. I picked up a dozen at my favorite sporting-good store in Watertown, along with a few other toys, and went to the register to check out and found Bushnell had a promo display. "Any laser range finders?" I asked. The gentleman handed me a nice compact handheld unit good to seven hundred yards—a nice unit, reasonably priced. "I'm a bow hunter," I added, and he lit right up. "Oh, do I have something for you," he said with a sly kind of chuckle. "Check this out—a laser range finder, eight to eighty yards, mounted right on your bow." Very nice, light too. I compared the two on a sign on the other side of the store, and they gave the same yardage read out. The price tag was reasonable as well, and he said, "And 20 percent off because of the promo day." Jenny just shook her head and went to the car to get the credit card. I took it to Randy's house for a little assistance mounting it on my bow. The bracket fit right behind the sight bar and mounted the unit right over my sights. "Man, that's perfect." Very little motion required: draw your bow, range your target, pick the pin accordingly, aim, and fire. Hopefully, take a little more of the guesswork out of those longer shots, especially in the heat of the moment, if you know what I mean.

I returned once again to my practice range and began sighting in with my broadheads. After two days of meticulous effort, I was able to consistently place my arrow in a six-inch square at seventy yards. I don't feel that's too bad for an old man.

It seems that time is flying. I have talked to Steve every week since that monumental day we were both drawn for a tag. We were both dancing on cloud nine. Final plans have been made, dates set, and the task of packing has been started. I shouldn't fail to mention that our dining entrées of freeze-dried food have been purchased. Everything was going smoothly until my flights were canceled—three times, I might add.

Well we are landing in Pittsburgh. I can only hope that my flight to Arizona will take off and hopefully on time. I'm in the air again; my departure was only forty minutes late but not too bad. This flight will take me all the way to Arizona.

On this leg of my journey, I managed to close my eyes and get some much-needed rest. My day started early, three thirty this morning and will go late tonight—driving to the rim, setting camp, and a three-hour time change.

To everyone's amazement, I have arrived in Arizona with all my gear. With just a short stop at Steve's house, we're on our way to the rim. It will take us about two and a half hours. Upon our arrival, we quickly made camp, and Steve took me into my watch, a nice spot in some ponderosa pines just below an oak brush plateau, a good transition area between feeding and bedding.

The evening brought dinner and a lot of catching up around our nonexistent campfire. Our camp was somewhat unsettled because someone was late getting in.

Four in the morning came early, but up we were. After a quick bowl of oatmeal and a hot cup of coffee, we departed camp in the dark for our first morning watch. I made the trek in just forty-five minutes, not bad my first time in alone and only the second time I've ever been there. I decided to make my stand between two giant boulders. It offered me a slight elevation in the pines. But before I could get my pack off, I heard a bugle; and my heart jumped. *My god, he's close.* And the rocks clicked as elks' hooves passed over them. It's still dark I can barely see. A white body appears, coming off the ridge, then another, and another. One to my right. He lets loose with a bugle. He's a bull for sure, but still all I can see are bodies; I can't see their heads, and it's too dark. Two more pass directly in front of me, no more than twenty yards away and broadside. I remained perfectly still and watched as more elk came down off the ridge. There were so many I couldn't count them all. The bull bugled again and again. My heart is racing, but I can't shoot because I can't see. I can't even see my pins. All I can see are white bodies. They passed my watch at a steady walk and didn't appear to be spooked at all, so I'm sure they were unaware of my presence. *Shit, why couldn't they have waited twenty minutes or so?* By then, I may have had enough light to make a shot. *Man, oh man, is this a good spot or what?* I laid down my bow for just a few minutes while I took off my pack and made my watch area ready for the next go around. Things remained quiet until 6:45 when a movement to my eleven o'clock got my attention *It's a bear!* Holy shit, and he isn't a cub either. I'll bet he's a four hundred pounder. A look with my field glasses gives him a brown tint to his black fur. He's sure nothing I want looking over my shoulder when I'm quartering an elk for packing out. I remained still at my watch until 9:20 when a movement again got my attention. *What is it? It's small and gray. An elk calf maybe?* A look with my field glasses confirmed it to be a mature whitetail buck with a very nice rack. Limbs prevented me from getting an accurate count, but I'm sure he was an eight or possibly a ten point.

Back at camp, Steve thought the bear was most likely a cinnamon bear. The buck was probably a muley, and he understood my frustration at the elk but relax this was just your first morning. I really hated to leave my morning watch with so much going on, so I returned early for my afternoon vigil. It was reasonably quiet except for a cow elk, who passed my watch about one hundred yards out. She passed at about 5:30 in enough light I could even see her head.

At 6:45, I began my first ascent back up to camp in the dark—where we managed a pleasant campfire, great coffee, and dined on chicken and rice. It was great tasting and easy to fix, just add boiling water and stir.

Steve asked me to leave my watch in a different direction and check for sign in this particular canyon. "No problem," I said. I would do it tomorrow morning. I got out my GPS and set the coordinance for camp, just in case I got turned around. After all, these are big woods out here, and it's a few miles between roads if you could find one, if you know what I mean.

Morning arrived as I was standing alert at my watch. It wasn't long until I heard noises on the ridge to my right. After listening and looking for about twenty minutes, I finally laid an eyeball on two elk. One was definitely a bull, and the other I'm not sure. They passed through at about one hundred yards out and headed in the same direction that the cow did the night before. Upon leaving my watch, I headed into the area I last saw the elk and found a lot of oak brush in the area. This could be a nice spot for an evening watch. I left the area and headed up the canyon that Steve asked me to check out the night before. I surveyed the area and found a lot of fresh sign, many droppings, and tracks. I also found a rub on a tree that had no branches for at least the first six feet, not one. Moving up the canyon, a crash about halfway up the wall froze me in my tracks. *A bull.* He's moving down and away from me. He probably saw me coming and decided it was time to get out of dodge. *You have my attention; is there anyone else in the area?* I stood for a while, just looking, then took a couple of steps and looked again. Bingo, halfway up, a cow is standing, looking in my direction. A closer look places another just below her. This one is a spike bull. He rose to his feet and just walked off. He didn't seem to be concerned. The cow offered me no shot, so I tried a cow chirp to bring her down. Again, she didn't seem to be at all alarmed but moved up the ridge instead of down. A look behind me produced another cow looking in my direction with her ears perked looking for the caller. *Just come a little closer. You're just out of range.* I'm afraid to call again. I'm sure she would spot me; I'm just too much in the open. She begins to move down off the ridge and stops behind a bush. I grasp the opportunity to move a little closer, trying to keep something between us, but she is able to move faster than I am and moves out of sight. This is a good spot to set up for a morning watch. I continued on checking out the rest of the canyon then headed for camp.

The evening hunt found us at a meadow a couple of miles away. Lots of sign, but we had little hope the elk would appear before it was completely dark. Our hunch was right, nothing appeared. I commented on how quiet it was—not even a bird or a slight breeze moving the trees, just dead still.

The next morning, I chose to return to my regular watch. I made the trek in the dark as usual. At my watch, my first chore is to load my bow then spray my clothes with a cover-up spray. To do this, I take off my shirt and jacket to be sure I get my back. My day pack caused me to sweat there, and I don't want any odor.

I just completed my chores when something was moving about eighty yards out. I grabbed my field glasses for a closer look. *Another bear. Oh shit, he's coming straight toward me.* I watched as he came closer with no hesitation. He has a definite destination, and it looks to be right between these two rocks. I lowered my glasses. I can see without them. He's within thirty yards and still coming. My heart is racing. I grabbed my bow with a quick look at my pins. The green twenty yards is the only one I can see. That was all I needed. He approached to within fifteen yards and stopped. My heart is about to leave my chest. I have a slight elevation advantage over him. If he comes straight on, I would be about four feet above him and no more than five yards away. He's still not moving. With my heart still pounding, I choose to talk, and maybe he'll leave. If he keeps coming, I'll have no choice left. "Bear, get out of here," I said in a normal voice as normal as possible. "Bear, get out of here." He did nothing other than turn and walk around the other rock. No growl, no wolfing, no popping of his teeth, or running. He just walked away. My senses remained razor sharp to any noise, and I kept an eye out above and to my rear in case he circled behind me. One bear surprise a day is enough. Before I returned to camp, I watched another small deer and listened to elk moving on the ridge to my right but no chances for a shot today.

Back at camp, Steve told me of the elk that passed his watch. Too far for a shot, but he did take a couple of pictures, and he also had a bear pass by his watch at a loping type of run. That was the first bear he had ever seen up here.

The next evening watch brought with it an early bugle at 5:20. I was encouraged and hopeful they would pass my watch. A mule deer eased through and takeable at two different spots. *Why can't elk do that?* I thought. As the evening wore on, the bull continued to bugle but moved away from my watch and seemed to move closer to camp.

Steve and I listened to his bugle all night. There seemed to be two, and, at one time, we figured they were about two hundred yards from camp. Sleeping was light that night, and when it came time to get up, it seemed he was heading back toward my watch.

The walk into my watch was the best I'd done yet. I managed to enter as quietly as possible. The map in my mind was very clear. Visibility was only feet, and it was easy to miss a landmark. Once off my established route, I was more apt to make unwanted noise.

After completing my chores at my watch, I listened to the bugling bull come and at times could hear rocks rolling and a limb snap as he came increasingly closer. His last bugle was 7:20, directly in front of me on the opposite ridge. At 9:30, the sun was warm, and I was sure he was bedded for the day, so I left my watch and headed for camp. I glanced at the opposite ridge after only moving twenty yards, just to see if anyone was near, and to my surprise, I picked up a cow just moving into the shade just about a hundred yards out. Once in the shade, she dropped to her knees and bedded up, looking directly in the direction I had to go. I decided to try a stalk. *Why not? The wind is in my favor, and she's going to see me anyway. It may be my last chance.* I dropped my pack and picked my steps to be sure of no noise. I had a good line with plenty of trees between me and her. My heart is beating a little harder with excitement. Five yards closer, I check. She shows no concern. Ten yards, I watched her ear twitch with the naked eye, as I moved behind another tree. Fifteen yards, a check with my field glasses locates another behind her, standing behind brush, looking the other way. Then up the canyon, about two hundred yards, a crashing of timber and rolling rocks. My bedded cow comes to her feet, and the other turns around. I catch a glimpse of a white body headed for the ridge. At the top, he lets out a bugle roar, and without hesitation, the two cows head up and away from me. I'm sure he was not spooked by me, but it is now clear for me to escape undetected.

On my way back to camp, I discovered fresh bear tracks in the mud. It's possible he came just a little too close for Mr. Bull's comfort.

Steve reported spooking some mule deer on the way in to his watch and also heard elk before ending his trek.

At camp, our domestic duties are really kept to a minimum. Eating freeze-dried food, there really is no mess to clean up—just add boiling water, let set for ten minutes, eat it, and throw away the package. No dishes to wash because all you did was boil water. On Wednesday, we had a real—cooked meal of spaghetti in one pot and heated the sauce and sausage in another; we also used spoons, covers, and a few other utensils. All of which had to be washed. Do this every day, and you have considerably increased the amount of water you need to carry in.

Steve made a colander out of a Styrofoam bowl to drain the spaghetti. I placed another bowl on top of it to keep it warm while we cooked more. A few minutes later, Steve told me to go ahead and eat mine while it was still warm. So he added sauce and sausage to the bowl and handed it to me. I sat down and began eating. A minute later, Steve said, "Where the hell is my colander?" "I don't know," I replied; but sauce is running down my arm. Oh my god, and he began to laugh. I guess I have the colander.

The evening watch started out slow until 6:00 when I heard movement on the ridge in front of me. Looking through the trees in front of me, I located an elk coming down. I quickly grabbed my bow and made ready. Its line of direction will pass by me at about thirty-five yards. My heart begins to pound, and excitement is taking over. I applied tension to the string of my bow. I'm ready to draw at any time. A closer look as the animal comes closer unveils a small rack. *Shit.* It's a bull. I have a cow tag. This one gets a you-can-pass-free card. I remained motionless and watched the young bull. As he changed direction and headed straight for me, he passed directly under my rock. I could have jumped on his back. I can't believe what I am seeing. He moved right between my rock and the big one to my right. At this point, he is broadside, just five yards from me and has no idea I am here. I'm stunned. I'm shocked and amazed at what just happened. Steve is sure to call me a liar.

Back at camp, I couldn't wait to tell my story. He was also amazed and excited. His evening, too, produced elk and deer sightings and unable to get a shot.

It was quiet that night, only a couple of bugles, unlike the night before when they went on all night.

Morning found me at my rock. There were bugles on the north ridge as I made my trek in, hoping they would stay on top until daylight came. Usually, the first two hours I remain standing to be ready quicker than if I sat down. After that, I sit and read and keep a sharp ear listening to what goes on around me and occasionally just look even if I don't hear anything. The squirrels are putting on quite a show today and making quite a lot of noise. I looked up behind me after a different noise blessed my ears and saw a cows deer and fawn coming down the ridge, headed right down where the bull went up. *This is unreal.* I was frozen as they passed, and I remained completely undetected. *Where is my camera at a time like this?* These deer only get to weigh about a hundred pounds full grown, and my dogs are twice the size of the fawn. What a picture that would have been!

Shortly after that, noise to the south draws my attention, then a brown object moving. Again, I grabbed my bow and made ready. The animal moves into clear view, and my heart again picks up the pace. It's my friend, Mr. Cinnamon Bear, moving slowly, checking the air; he passed the same thirty-five-yard opening the bull elk did and looked like he was going to pass straight through until he changed direction and headed toward the rock to my right. My heart pounds as he passed me at just fifteen yards. I'm quiet and still. He walked right to the rock and sniffed at the cave and started to move away. Almost out of sight, he turned and headed back. I think he wants to go up the same trail the cows deer came down. I don't think that's a good idea at all. At fifteen yards I spoke again. "Bear, get out of here." He stopped. "Bear, get out of here." He didn't appear to be alarmed but turned 180 degrees and went around the other side and out of sight. My bow remained in my hands for at least the next half hour, and I kept a sharp eye behind me. Again, I wondered, *Where is my camera?* Back at camp, I guarantee it will be in my pack tonight.

The next night and morning were quiet—no action at all, not even any bugling at night. It makes you wonder where they went. They're not like caribou, which migrate through here today and are gone tomorrow. They should remain in the same general area unless driven out.

The afternoon was hot, I mean hot. At camp, you moved into the shade just to bear it. A record temperature in the valley of 107 degrees. I told you, it's hot.

Usually, we're ready to head for our watches by 3:00 PM, but today it's hot; and we're lazy, so it was four before we were ready. Steve decided to sit in the canyon southwest of my location tonight, hoping for some action.

I left camp with my bow over my shoulder as usual and began my journey down the road. Once in the woods, travel becomes much slower to maintain a quiet surrounding. I reached the bottom of the ridge and headed through the pines and across the flats when I heard a thunder of hooves to my right. I jerked my head and saw two cows charging toward my location and right behind them a bull. He, too, appeared to be all out. Something has them spooked. My bow rolled off my shoulder and into my left hand. An arrow came out of my quiver, and, my knock headed for the string with my right hand trembling, I completed the task and attached my release and drew my bow while swinging in a ninety-degree circle. The elk are passing my location now. I gave a quick *blatt, blatt*; the lead cow's head snapped in my direction. I gave the distance a quick forty-yard guess, hit her with my third pin directly behind the shoulder, and fired. The elk tore up the ground in a desperate attempt to escape. After the arrow went *crack*, I quickly stooped and looked through the trees, looking for my arrow in the elk or some indication of my hit. I saw nothing, and the bull disrupted my line of sight. I watched as the elk crossed the dry creek bed and go up the hill out of sight. My heart pounds as I try to grasp the last ten seconds. *Did I miss? Did I hit a tree? I don't think so.* I quickly checked the downed log on the other side of the flats. Nothing. I'll check the logs the elk crossed at the dry creeks. *Bingo.* I found the red trail markers left by the fleeing elk. I left my hat here and checked the next log, more blood here; I left my day pack. I should wait and not push, give her a chance to lie down. I quickly headed up the canyon toward the area Steve was going to sit. I moved up the canyon for about fifteen minutes then began calling, "Steve." Three or four calls later, I see him. He doesn't appear to know I'm coming, so I yell, "Hey." Steve looked in my direction, and I gave him an arm motion to come. "I hear you; I'm coming," Steve said. "Man, are you excited? What happened?" After listening to my story, he asked if I saw the hit. I said, "No, but I have blood." "Did you find the arrow?" Again, I said no. We quickly returned to where I left my hat and day pack and began the task of trailing my game uphill. Steve said he didn't like the way she's moving up. I agreed. At times, we found blood on both sides of the trail when she passed between bushes. With this, we were sure the arrow passed straight through. The trail became harder and harder to find as she continued to climb. It's now after 6:00 PM, and we have lost our trail. We're sure she has clotted, and the bleeding stopped. We circled the area before heading back. We estimated that we traveled between three to four-tenths of a mile back to our gear. As we trailed her, we never found my arrow. It must be somewhere back at the beginning. We retrieved our packs, and I attempted to find the location where I shot. Twice, I said, "This doesn't look right." Then I found a log that looked like the log I first checked. She was around here, I'm sure, and here's my arrow just lying on the ground. I carefully picked it up by the knock. It's completely covered with red blood, no bubble rings; and it's just red, not dark red like a liver hit. There is also some tallow on the shaft. All of these indications, along with her going uphill, lead us to believe I hit her high in the no zone above the lungs. The good news is she shouldn't be affected by it other than a clean cut that will heal.

We decided to cut our morning hunt short our final day because of our task to pack before we head down to the valley. It's hard to believe our hunt is over as we pull out of camp for the last time, leaving it just as we found it. As it's been said, "Leave only footprints and take only memories." Memories of all the elk my first morning. Cows deer Steve had never seen here before. The bear so close I was trembling in my boots. The bull that passed within five yards of me and never knew I was there. The many shows put on by the squirrels at my watch, along with the hummingbird hovering twelve inches from my face. Our camp life was truly half our trip, sitting by the fire remembering past hunts and other trips and laughing over spaghetti. As far as my shot, in the heat of the moment, I made a snap decision on the distance of my shot, and it was wrong. I just wasn't lucky this time. After all, it's never been like shooting at a target, but it will take one hell of a trip to ever come close to this one. Thanks Steve.

Terry

Chapter 18

OUR BIGGEST BUCKS

Terry's Tale

It was one of those beautiful fall days, midway through bow season, when the temperatures were just right. Cool, but not cold. You're comfortable wearing light camo and don't need bulky clothes to be able to sit a stand for more than an hour or two. This is the time of year I can truly relax and enjoy the woods. I can sit in one of my stands and enjoy what goes on around me.

This fall, I had decided to change the stand I'm sitting in every night. This will give me a good idea where the deer are moving. So far, the season is eight days old, and I have seen as many as six and as few as two each evening but no bucks. Tonight, I planned to sit in a hemlock tree on a major runway that leads to some apples and white oak trees. I expect to see some action here and hopefully a buck.

It's late afternoon, and time to get dressed. Jenny and I change our clothes at our camper and decide which stand we'll sit. Jenny decides to watch the cornfield. I told her of my plans and where I'd be in case she needs me.

The walk to my stand is maybe a half mile. The trail is wide, and I keep it mowed with my walk behind brush hog. The result is a quiet approach, disturbing nothing in the surrounding area. The walk was uneventful. I heard nothing and saw nothing. I attached my bow to the drop line and climbed to my perch. With my bow loaded, I took my seat and got comfortable. I was only perched maybe fifteen minutes when the action started. A motion to my left, a deer soon comes into clear view. It heads straight for the apple tree thirty yards away. I watched it feed for a few minutes and decided to take a closer look. I pulled out my field glasses, and to my amazement, I discovered a pair of spikes, maybe three to three and a half inches long. I decided I really didn't want him doing any of the breeding and passing those spikes on to another generation. My bow came to full draw, and I began looking for an opening. A twig here, a branch there, I just couldn't find a clean shot. So I reached for my grunt tube and gave it two short blows, and action immediately came from a different direction—twigs snapping and the sound of a deer loping right at me. It's a small deer, maybe one of this year's fawns. Its ears are alert and looking for whoever gave it the call. It continually searched while still moving and ended up maybe five feet from my tree. The spike buck that I wanted to move is still feeding under the apple tree. I don't dare to call again; I'll surely get spotted by the smaller deer. I'm forced to remain still and hope the smaller deer moves on. No such luck. The spike finished feeding and disappeared, never giving me an opportunity to make my shot. The smaller deer stayed close to my stand until just before dark. I really don't like to spook a deer near my watch if possible. When all was quiet, I descended my tree and quietly left the area.

I returned to the camper, and Jenny was waiting for me. Her evening was completely quiet—no action at all, just peace and quiet. You can't even hear the phone ring out here.

When we returned the next night, Jenny opted to try a stand on a hemlock ridge in the little swamp. I decided to return to the stand I sat in last night. Maybe the spike buck I saw last night will return. I approached the area as slowly as I could, and without making much noise, I eliminated a few twigs and branches between the apple tree and my stand. If he comes back, I have a better chance than I did last night. I climbed my tree and began my vigil.

The evening was uneventful except for one twig snap about an hour before dark. My attention was focused in that direction, but nothing developed. About ten minutes before dark, I lowered my bow to the ground. Another twig snapped, closer than before. Maybe I'll wait just a few more minutes. I raised my bow, knocked an arrow, and waited. Soon, another snap in the same direction. Now motion narrows my focus even more. It's a deer. It moves closer, and I'm sure it's a mature one. *Holy shit! It's a buck, and he ain't no spikehorn either,* (excuse my English). His rack towers over his head, and his rack is well beyond his ears. If he continues in the same direction, he'll pass right in front of me. Slowly, he moves gracefully in every step and unaware of my presence. He stopped behind a small evergreen tree. *Draw now*, I thought; and I raised my bow and came to full draw in one smooth motion. The arrow slid back over the arrow rest without a sound. My anchor felt perfect as I settled in. I turned my complete focus to the pink top pin on my sight bar, and the huge buck took two more steps.

My heart is pounding in my chest. *Calm down and do it right*, I thought. He stopped just twelve yards in front of me and looked away. Perfect! There was nothing between him and me, the pink pin dropped to just behind his shoulder, and I fired. At two hundred and forty-seven feet per second, the arrow hit its mark before the buck had a chance to react. The arrow passed completely through him before he squatted then bounded from the area. My heart is still pounding, and now I'm beginning to shake from the adrenaline rush. Daylight is fading fast, and I need to find my arrow. I descended my tree and quickly found my arrow. It was completely covered with blood, no tallow or green gut stuff. I'm sure it was a good hit. I left the arrow where it lay, grabbed my bow, and left the area.

Back at the camper, I ask Jenny if she had any luck. "Not a thing," she replied. "How about you?" "Jenny, I shot a monster!" "Oh yea, right!" she replied. "Jenny, I did. I really did, and we need to find him!" We grabbed a roll of toilet paper and the lantern from the camper and headed back. Jay, my neighbor, was in his backyard, so I gave him a yell. "Jay, grab your flashlight and come on; I hit a big one." "All right," he said. "Just give me a minute." As we walked down the trail, I told them my story. Jenny and Jay were both excited and couldn't wait to find him. At my watch, the arrow was the first on our agenda. "He went that way," I said as I pointed. Sometimes, the first blood is the hardest to find but not this time. We had a good trail to follow, and Jenny left a toilet paper trail as we went deeper into the dark. This will help us find our way out. This swamp is two miles wide and four miles long, and after dark, it's easy to get turned around. Our track led us to a fine eight-point buck with a sixteen-inch spread, and he scored one hundred and sixteen Pope and Young points at two-and-a-half-years old. He weighed one hundred and seventy-two pounds. This is the biggest buck I have ever taken. It's never been important to me to take a big one. Just being there and enjoying the adventure is enough. But you can be sure I won't forget this one any time too soon.

Jenny's Tale

The hunting season is in full swing here in upstate New York. The bucks are starting to rut. I have been finding scrapes and a few rubs around the swamp. Jenny is having a ruff time of it this year. She has been to the doctor several times, and they have diagnosed her with . . . diferfiseiouts . . . diverfisious . . . you know, she has a sore foot. It's been hard for her to walk any distance, though she still wants to hunt. Unable to go deep into the swamp like before, she is confined to hunt close to home. We have four stands she can pick from. One on the lower forty, one on our southeast corner, another on our archery course, and the last one in the hard woods.

I found a real nice buck rub in the area of three of these stands, so there is a buck here somewhere.

We have had quite a lot of rain lately and for Jenny, with a cast on, it's even harder to get out. The die-hard that she is, she puts a plastic bag on her foot when she goes out. Why not put a rubber boot on, you ask? We tried that. It didn't work. They don't make one big enough.

This year, I'm using my twenty-gauge shotgun during gun season because my 06 had a misfire as I went to remove a round from the chamber. To open the bolt, you must take the safety off. When I did, it went off and sent a round into the ground. Thankfully, we always practice our gun safety because you just never know when something will happen. My gunsmith replaced a worn part in the safety, but I still don't feel comfortable with it. I'll probably trade it before next year. Jenny has a real nice 243 bolt-action sporting, a three-to-nine-power scope. A real nice rifle for her, and she is a real good shot with it too.

I'm retired from construction, so I'm always around home doing something or headed for a stand. On this day, the sun is finally shining. To take advantage of that, Jenny left work early. She said she wanted to sit in the hard woods. I said I'd be about a quarter of a mile to her south. We both carry radios, so if I hear her shoot, I'd turn mine on, and she would do the same if she heard me shoot.

I took up my vigil early, about four o'clock, and didn't have any action at all. But around six, I was sure I heard Jenny shoot. I reached in my pocket and turned on my radio and waited. Nothing! I waited about a half an hour and still nothing. Then I became concerned. I was sure it was her that fired. I climbed down from my tree and headed in her direction, really not sure what had happened. Did she fall? I hope not. Did she miss? I don't think so. Or wasn't it her that shot? As I got closer to her watch, she called me on the radio. "Ter, are you there?" "Yea, I'm within two hundred yards of you now." "Are you going to come help me with my *buck?*" she replied. "I had to go back to the house to get new batteries for my radio. The buck is in the trail; I'm bringing the four wheeler and trailer."

I approached to find a beautiful, mature, eight point, three-and-a-half-years old, and one hundred and fifty-three pound buck. After the ninety-day drying period, he measured fifteen inches inside spread and scored 105 Boone and Crockett points. She took him right in the neck and dropped him in his tracks. That's my Jenny!

Chapter 19

OUR WEDDING

On June 8, 2002, Jenifer and I were married at sunset, overlooking Lake Ontario, high on the side of a hill between the harbors of Henderson and Sackets. It was, as one guest put it, the most beautiful wedding she has ever been to. You can even hear the birds singing in the background. Because it was a sunset wedding, the reception was held before the service. I chose to say just a few words to express the way I felt on this most wonderful day in our lives.

"We want to thank Jenifer's mom for giving us this party today; we really appreciate it. Keith and Jaime, our attendants, for everything they have done to make this weekend so wonderful and to all our family and friends—your presence here makes our day complete.

"A wise man once said, 'If you want to be seen, stand up. If you want to be heard, speak up. If you want to be appreciated, sit down and shut up. Well, that's not going to happen here today.

"Jenifer and I have known each other for over sixteen years, and in those sixteen years, we raised my youngest daughter together; we built a new home for ourselves in a place we call paradise. We've traveled the United States from Maine to Hawaii, cruised the Caribbean, the Bahamas, and Mexico. We've climbed mountains in the Adirondacks, enjoyed canoeing, camping, and backpacking. We've also ridden the wild rapids of the Colorado River in Colorado. We've hunted bear in Canada when the bugs were so bad Jenny's eye was swelled shut. We've hunted elk in Wyoming when we were left out on a mountain all night with no tent, no sleeping bag, no food, no nothing, at 9,600 feet on the last week of September. The point that I'm trying to make is that on this day, I will marry my very best friend."